"I have long admired David deSilva's capacity to help a broad audience hear Revelation's ancient message and its contemporary challenges. His beautiful writing provides the honey that makes historical and literary detail pleasant to consume. Here, deSilva updates his work to engage emerging threats to Christian witness, specifically cultural and political allegiances that undermine faithfulness to Jesus."

—GREG CAREY, associate dean for the Lancaster Campus and professor of New Testament, Moravian University School of Theology

"Many people struggle to see the practical relevance that Revelation has for today. Unfortunately, many popular books on the subject merely add to the struggle, as they tend to interpret Revelation's mysterious symbols and figurative language as having only to do with far-off, distant future events. But in this book, New Testament scholar David deSilva offers a better—indeed, a more faithful—approach to reading Revelation.

Living in an Unholy Empire takes readers back to the first century, where the early church found itself in the midst of very difficult sociopolitical trials and temptations. However, deSilva offers so much more than just a lesson in church history. By situating Revelation within its original context, he invites us to more accurately reflect upon the challenges of today and to consider how we can be faithful to Jesus in a world dominated by unholy powers. With scholarly insight and pastoral clarity, deSilva demonstrates how Revelation's message offers truth and grace to a modern world that desperately needs healing and peace. Every Christian needs to read this book."

—MATTHEW L. HALSTED, associate professor of biblical studies, Eternity Bible College

"The previous edition of deSilva's book, *Unholy Allegiances: Heeding Revelation's Warning*, was among the must-read volumes for Christians trying to make sense of Revelation, so this revised edition is surely welcomed. The discussions of Rome and the imperial cult, as well as John's portrayal of Jesus, have been significantly expanded. Complementary illustrations continue to accompany its readable text. Recent archaeological discoveries like the graffiti in the Smyrna agora are discussed. And interpretative adjustments are made, such as adding a fifth feature to the pattern of the seven oracles or revising the translation of the Calendar Decree of Asia. The addition of a chapter relating Revelation to politics and Christian witness is both incisive and timely, given the highly politicized state of the American church today. With this update, deSilva continues to bring clarity and insight to reading Revelation."

—MARK WILSON, director, Asia Minor Research Center, Antalya, Turkey

Living in an

UNHOLY EMPIRE

Living in an UNHOLY EMPIRE

REVELATION AND THE CALL TO A HIGHER ALLEGIANCE

DAVID A. DESILVA

HENDRICKSON

Living in an Unholy Empire: Revelation's Call to a Higher Allegiance

Published by Hendrickson Publishers
Hendrickson Publishers, LLC
3 Centennial Drive
Peabody, Massachusetts 01960
www.hendricksonpublishers.com

ISBN 979-8-4005-2344-1
Kindle: 979-8-4005-2345-8
ePub: 979-8-4005-2346-5
Apple: 979-8-4005-2347-2

First edition published in 2013 as *Unholy Allegiances: Heeding Revelation's Warning.*

Translations by the author are marked "AT."

Cover design by Karol Bailey.

Printed in the United States of America

35 34 33 32 31 30 29 28 27 26
10 9 8 7 6 5 4 3 2 1

Library of Congress Control Number 2026941397

To my mother, Dorothy Alberta de Silva,
in honor of her 90th birthday

Contents

Illustrations

Preface

Many books on Revelation written for a general audience push some author's new and innovative decoding of Revelation's "predictions" in terms of current developments in world politics. Often this includes some forecast of what the author believes will come to pass in the readers' near future based on his or her alignment of Revelation with current events. One can also find such books at closeout prices ten years later after the ongoing course of history has proven their contents false and rendered them irrelevant, though by this time the author will have already published his or her next exposé of the end times.

I wrote this book for people who are no longer, or who have never been, satisfied with this kind of speculative, fanciful, often manipulative approach to Revelation. I wrote this book for those who suspect that Revelation does have an important word to speak to the churches today, but also that John's concern is not to provide a playbook for the end times. I also wrote this book for people like those who were captivated by Harold Camping's predictions of the return of Jesus and the rapture of the faithful in May (and then October) of 2011, or by Gerald Flurry's trumpeting in 2020 that the COVID-19 pandemic would shake the European Economic Union back down to the requisite number of ten (in fulfillment of Rev. 17:12–14), or by myriad other "prophecy experts" who make of Revelation a Christian Ouija board for prognosticating the future. Surely it is time to take John's word to John's congregations in Asia Minor more seriously, and to study the book—in Harold Camping's own words after finally admitting his failure—"even more fervently . . . not to find dates, but to be more faithful in understanding."[1]

1. "Letter from Harold Camping to the 'Family Radio Family,'" *Charisma News*, March 7, 2012. Archived here (accessed December 22, 2025): https://web.archive.org/web/20120310001154/http://charismanews.com/us/32958-harold-camping-admits-rapture-prediction-was-sinful-statement.

My own starting point for reading and interpreting Revelation is to ask what John's word would have meant to Christians in the seven churches located in the Roman province of Asia Minor in the late first century CE and how it would have challenged them in their setting. On this basis, I invite readers to ponder how John would analyze and address our contemporary situation, what he would identify as the significant challenges to preserving faithful response and witness, and how he would change our outlook on the major features of our own landscape such that we become more inclined to overcome those challenges.

Primarily, I wrote this book for people like those who populate my own church and who participate together in small groups or Sunday morning Christian education programs. While I am a New Testament scholar by training and profession, my primary goal for my work is to help people in churches, whether ministry staff or laity, listen to Scripture more intently and intentionally, and work to discern its guidance for the formation of disciples and faith communities. I believe that much popular writing on Revelation has hindered people from such genuine listening and discernment, and so I am particularly passionate about communicating the fruits of scholarly study of Revelation to the people who gather around this book as "the Word of the Lord" alongside the rest of the writings in the Christian canon.

If this book is well illustrated, it is in large measure due to the generosity and efforts of a number of individuals who went out of their way to help, for which I am profoundly grateful, particularly Mr. Brad Nelson of Classical Numismatic Group, LLC (cngcoins.com) and Ms. Francesca Passarelli of Numismatica Ars Classica AG (arsclassicacoins.com), who graciously gave me permission to use images of coins depicting facets of Roman imperial ideology.

I have traveled repeatedly to the archaeological sites of the seven cities whose Christian residents were addressed by John and am grateful to those in the travel companies that made that possible for me—Mr. Abdullah Gur of Meander Travel (Kuşadası, Türkiye), Mr. Levent Oral of Tutku Educational Travel (Izmir, Türkiye), and Mr. James Ridgway of Educational Opportunities Tours (Lakeland, Florida). The material in the first edition of this book took shape as a series of presentations prepared for travelers on cruises organized by Educational Opportunities Tours, and I am particularly indebted to Mr. James Ridgway and to his father before him, Dr. Jim Ridgway, for the occasions they provided both to hone my thoughts on Revelation and experience several of the sites pertinent to Revelation in connection with these cruises.

As in all my writing endeavors, I am also grateful to the trustees and the administrators of Ashland Theological Seminary, a graduate division of Ashland University, whose support of my work is a token of their commitment to educating not only the students who enroll in our degree programs but also all who are a part of the Christian church.

Abbreviations

Old Testament

Gen.	Genesis
Exod.	Exodus
Lev.	Leviticus
Num.	Numbers
Deut.	Deuteronomy
1 Kgs.	1 Kings
2 Kgs.	2 Kings
Ps. (Pss.)	Psalm(s)
Prov.	Proverbs
Isa.	Isaiah
Jer.	Jeremiah
Ezek.	Ezekiel
Dan.	Daniel
Hos.	Hosea
Jon.	Jonah
Zech.	Zechariah
Mal.	Malachi

New Testament

Matt.	Matthew
Rom.	Romans
1–2 Cor.	1–2 Corinthians
Gal.	Galatians
Eph.	Ephesians
Phil.	Philippians
1–2 Thess.	1–2 Thessalonians

1 Tim.	1 Timothy
Heb.	Hebrews
Jas.	James
Rev.	Revelation

Apocrypha

Bar.	Baruch
1 Macc.	1 Maccabees
2 Macc.	2 Maccabees
4 Macc.	4 Maccabees
Sg. Three	Song of the Three Young Men
Tob.	Tobit
Wis.	Wisdom of Solomon

Dead Sea Scrolls

1QH	Thanksgiving Hymns
1QM	*Milḥamah* or War Scroll

Greek and Latin Works

Aelius Aristides

Or.	*Orationes*

Dio Cassius

Hist.	*Historia Romana*

Josephus

J.W.	*Jewish War*

Pausanias

Descr.	*Description of Greece*

Tacitus

Agr.	*Agricola*
Hist.	*Historiae*

Virgil

Aen.	*Aeneid*

LCL	Loeb Classical Library

1

Debunking Popular Myths About Revelation

I first read Revelation when I was thirteen years of age, after I had read through the four Gospels and Acts. I suppose that, like most teenagers, I was allergic to the feeling that I was being "lectured," and so the letters of Paul and his fellow apostles did not hold such immediate appeal as the narratives. Revelation, however, was gripping. Its fantastic and mysterious images, its cosmic scope, its astounding pronouncements about the stakes involved in keeping or failing to keep its "word"—Revelation was well crafted to sink its hooks into the reader's mind.

As I sought guidance for understanding this "word," and thereby having a chance at keeping it, the people whose guidance I sought tended to have one of two somewhat extreme reactions. I went first to the rector of the Episcopal church of which I was a member. He was always open to discussing the faith and the Scriptures, and I had typically found him to be a source of great encouragement. On this occasion, however, he admitted that he had little exposure to the book, and so he took me to the church library, sat me down with the final volume of the old Interpreter's Bible, and essentially wished me luck. Then there was my maternal grandmother's older sister, whom I simply called "Aunt." Though raised Baptist, she had joined the Seventh-day Adventist Church and knew exactly what Revelation was about, from beginning to end. She read about it constantly, and my display of interest prompted a steady flow of conversation and sharing of "literature" over the space of a decade.

In one setting, Revelation was beyond the purview even of the religious professionals. In the other, it was the interpretive key to the whole canon, the focus for study on the part of every active layperson. In both settings, Revelation was a kind of Pandora's box. In the first setting, it wasn't something that one tended to open. While texts from Revelation were occasionally read as part of the lectionary cycle, these tended to be only from those relatively safe portions that spoke of the state of the blessed (e.g., Rev. 7:9–17 or 21:1–6 on All Saints' Day). But for the most part, the contents of Revelation were kept safely locked away. In the second setting, every church member was a Pandora, eagerly opening the box and allowing its contents to overrun the world around them, as they went off chasing the beast in this or that political figure, following the whore to this or that country, seeing the gallop of the four horsemen in this or that series of news briefs.

As a result, the witness of John's voice has largely been lost to the churches. Where Revelation is tucked away rather than read and studied regularly, its silence in the church is obvious. Where Revelation is avidly consumed as a playbook for the end times (in which the readers of whatever period inevitably believe themselves to be living), John's own voice is equally silent, this time trumped by the voice of the interpreter who uses Revelation to speak of things about which John had never imagined, and who, in the process, loses sight of those things that John passionately sought to communicate to the church. The latter approach has largely dominated public discourse about Revelation, extending its reach through all available media, including a best-selling series of novels and a not-quite-as-successful series of movies.

As people get caught up in the imagery of Revelation and try to find answers to these questions, they often fall headlong into some mistakes, forgetting some of the most basic and most important principles of studying the Bible. In regard to Revelation, in particular, I find many popular speakers and writers, and the many more who follow them, to have been led astray by three basic fallacies—three myths, if you will—about Revelation.

Myth #1: Revelation Is About Us

The misconception that Revelation is about *us* may spring from a wholesome desire to find the relevance of this book for us. Or perhaps it springs out of that general self-centeredness that most of us never quite get over entirely. We often forget, in our rush to turn to Scripture to hear a word "for us," that all these texts originally spoke a word "for them," that is, for communities of faith removed from us by more than nineteen centuries, and that we are the secondary beneficiaries of the pastoral guidance initially intended for them.

John gives some cues that should remind us, as attentive readers, that this book is not in fact about us. In particular, he signals that Revelation is to be read as a letter—one that turns out to be, like Paul's letters, a pastoral intervention in the form of a letter. After an introductory paragraph in which John does not speak in his own voice but in an impersonal voice comparable to the openings of the writings of other biblical prophecies (compare Rev. 1:1–3 with Isa. 1:1 and Jer. 1:1–3), John's own voice sounds out in words that recall the opening of other early Christian letters: "John to the seven congregations that are in Asia: Grace to you and peace" (Rev. 1:4 AT[1]). The standard formula with which letters began in the Hellenistic and Roman periods—"sender to addressees, greetings"—is clearly present.[2] John even uses a typically Christian modification of the basic "greeting" (Greek, *chairein*) already familiar from the letters of Paul and Peter—"Grace [Greek, *charis*] to you and peace."[3]

John provides an important reading cue here, signaling that Revelation is to be read within the framework of a letter addressed explicitly to seven real communities of Christians in the Roman province of Asia Minor (now westernmost Türkiye). This is reinforced by the divine command that John hears: "Write down in a scroll what you see, and send it to the seven congregations, to Ephesus and to Smyrna and to Pergamum and to Thyatira and to Sardis and to Philadelphia and to Laodicea" (1:11 AT). John would therefore have intended Revelation to be understood by them, to shape their perceptions of their everyday realities, and to motivate particular responses to their immediate circumstances.

FIGURE 1.1. The locations of the churches in Roman Asia addressed by John. (Courtesy of Rusty Russell, Bible History Online; www.bible-history.com.)

1. "AT" indicates author's translation.

2. Examples of this ancient convention are conveniently found in Acts 15:23; 23:26; Jas. 1:1. Further examples can be found in the books of the Apocrypha, e.g., 1 Macc. 10:18, 25; 11:30, 32; 12:6, 20; 2 Macc. 11:16, 22, 27, 34.

3. Compare Rom. 1:7; 1 Cor. 1:3; 2 Cor. 1:3, etc.

The pervasive use of the number seven in Revelation suggests that the seven churches are, in some way, representative of the achievements and challenges facing churches across the Mediterranean in the first century and across the globe throughout church history, such that the words addressed to these seven congregations also speak to churches beyond that circle. This is comparable to the fact that Paul's letters have continued to give theological and formational guidance far beyond the original settings in which Paul sought to intervene. Nevertheless, these seven specifically named congregations were also seven real Christian assemblies (or clusters of assemblies) facing particular difficulties and situations, whose response to their world John wanted to affect profoundly. A grounded and responsible reading of Revelation begins with reading it first as we would read Paul's Letters to the Galatians or Philippians or the Letters of the Elder (1–3 John)—namely, as a piece of communication that reveals its meaning and message most fully when we immerse ourselves in the contexts and conversations of its ancient audience, when we exercise ourselves to understand it as a pastoral word to them in the midst of their concerns and circumstances. The primary obstacle to understanding Revelation in the twenty-first century is the modern reader's distance from the environment, experiences, and knowledge that John and his congregations shared and that made Revelation intelligible to John's immediate audiences.

Myth #2: What Revelation Reveals Is Our Future

A second reading cue emerges even earlier in the book, as an anonymous voice declares, "Privileged is the one who is reading out loud, and those who are listening to, the words of this prophecy, and who are keeping the things written in it" (Rev. 1:3 AT; see also 22:7, 10, 18, 19). The contents are presented as "the words of this prophecy" (1:3 AT), a term that, for better or worse, modern English speakers tend to equate first with prediction, communicating murky oracles looking off into the distant future, as in the prophecies of Nostradamus that supposedly spoke of events centuries after the time of the speaker. This understanding of prophecy as prediction has given rise to three of the major schools of thought in regard to interpreting Revelation—the historicist, futurist, and preterist approaches to the book's "prophecies."

The *historicist* approach reads Revelation as a prediction of events spanning the period between John's own time and the future, end-time coming again of Jesus and the creation of the new heavens and new earth. The visions reveal the course of history in the long in-between, with the interpreters generally locating themselves toward the end of that span.

The *futurist* approach regards Revelation as consisting of mostly yet-unfulfilled predictions. Some of Revelation may pertain to events contemporary with its author ("what is," 1:19), but the vast majority of Revelation's material speaks of the end-time future ("what is to take place after this," 1:19). Thus while futurist interpreters also generally view themselves as living near the beginning of the "last days," they tend to regard most of Revelation's predictions as still ahead of them. The oracles to the seven churches are often read as a means of bridging the distance between John and the present generation, with each congregation representing a broad period in the history of the church.[4] The futurist reading allows for the highest degree of literalism, for example, the expectation that a third of earth's trees and grass will perish. Since this has never actually happened, the historicist interpreter must temper the literal sense somehow in order to connect the sounding of that first trumpet (8:7) with some past event, while the futurist interpreter is free to imagine the scene of destruction more literally.[5]

The *preterist* reading gives more weight to John's consistent emphasis that "the time is near" (1:3; 22:10) and that the visions are imminently relevant ("what must soon take place," 1:1). Thus this approach reads Revelation's prophecies as fulfilled in events of the distant past, whether as a prediction of events from John's time to the establishment of the Christian state under Constantine (with the millennium commencing with the legalization and empowerment of the Christian religion) or even events culminating in the destruction of Jerusalem (represented, in this reading, by Babylon) in 70 CE. Some preterist interpreters go so far as to identify the second coming of Christ with the fall of Jerusalem.

4. Regarding each church as representative of the whole church in a particular era grossly caricatures the periods of church history so described. See "Extended Note: The Seven Oracles as Epochs of Church History" in chapter 6.

5. Some futurist interpreters insist not only that we are in a better position to understand Revelation in our time than John's original audiences were, but that we can have a better grasp of what John himself was seeing but couldn't articulate effectively given his comparatively primitive experiences. Hal Lindsey, for example, suggested that what John described as locusts with breastplates were actually assault helicopters and what he had described as horses spouting fire and smoke were mobile ballistic missile launchers (*There's a New World Coming: A Prophetic Odyssey* [Bantam, 1975], 126). When the interpreter thinks he or she has a better grasp of John's *visions* than even John himself did, an important line has been crossed rather than honored.

All three approaches are based on the assumption that by "prophecy" John primarily indicates that he is communicating predictions about specific events that will yet unfold at some point in his first audience's future, and that this is the interpretative key to the book. They differ only in terms of the time frame of that fulfillment. But is "prophecy" essentially "prediction"?

To answer this, we turn to the prophetic utterances of the Hebrew Bible and to the phenomenon of prophecy within the New Testament and early Christian worship. While such prophecy could include a predictive element, it was also—and perhaps primarily—a declaration of God's action in the present or an announcement of God's evaluation of the present actions of God's people, diagnosing problems and calling for realignment with God's values. Prophecy is essentially a "word of the Lord" breaking into the situation of the Lord's people who need guidance or encouragement or a call to repentance and recommitment.

"Prophecy" was a regular experience in the worship life of the Pauline churches. The new pouring out of the Holy Spirit upon God's people resulted in a renewal of the possibility of hearing the divine voice given utterance by the Spirit through the mouths of those who were possessed by the Spirit (Rom. 12:6; 1 Cor. 12:10, 28–29; Eph. 4:11). While there are certainly elements of prediction involved in some prophetic utterances (for example, 1 Tim. 1:18), the primary element appears to have been "edification," the revelation of a supramundane perspective that invited a radical reorientation to one's circumstances, practices, or pursuits. This clearly emerges from Paul's own understanding of the prophetic gift at work (when working at its best) in the Corinthian churches (1 Cor. 14:3–4, 23–25, 29–31). In John's situation, Jezebel's own activity as a "prophet" involves chiefly "teaching" (Rev. 2:20) in regard to the boundaries of acceptable Christian practice (although, in her case, those boundaries are considerably wider than John would affirm).

In Revelation, the seven "letters" to the seven churches are a prime example of early Christian prophecy in action. These would be more appropriately called the seven "oracles" to the seven churches, for these communications do not begin with the familiar letter-opening formula. Rather, after John is commanded to "write" down something for each congregation's "angel," the actual message to the congregation begins in a manner much more reminiscent of prophetic oracles. The formula familiar from the Hebrew prophets—"Thus says the Lord"—is readily heard in "The First and the Last says this" (Rev. 2:8 AT) or "The Son of God says this" (2:18 AT). The risen and glorified Lord speaks a word to the churches through the prophet

John, affirming their strengths, diagnosing their weaknesses, calling them to faithful action, threatening judgment upon the recalcitrant, and promising favor for the penitent and faithful. In short, they do precisely what so much of the prophetic writings of the Old Testament sought to do for the communities of Israel and Judah.

Where one of the Hebrew prophets spoke of the future, he often limited the prediction to the immediately forthcoming future, not the distant future: "Forty days more, and Nineveh shall be overthrown" (Jon. 3:4); "There shall be neither dew nor rain these years" (1 Kgs. 17:1); and the like. The point was not prediction of distant events, but warning of imminent events that had bearing on the here and now of the prophet's audience. John remains within this range, seen in his persistent emphasis on the "imminence" of the confrontations and events he narrates and his conviction that he speaks about "what must soon take place" (Rev. 22:6; see also 1:3, 19; 4:1; 22:7, 10, 12, 20).

The modern "Bible prophecy expert" holds that everything presented in the Bible as a forecast of some future event must be fulfilled at some point. If the "prophecies" of Revelation did not match up with historical events or figures during the first or second century, they *must* at some point have such a match. This tenet, however, ignores the primary purpose of prophecy, which is not to give hard and fast statements about an unchangeable future but to evoke faithful response. The book of Jonah provides an instructive example. Jonah was sent to Nineveh simply to proclaim: "Forty days more, and Nineveh shall be overthrown" (Jon. 3:4). In response to this announcement concerning the imminent future, the city's inhabitants repented and turned to God, with the result that God spared the city (3:10). Jonah, like the prophecy expert, was still watching "to see what would become of the city" (4:5) and was bitterly disappointed that the prediction was not fulfilled. God's purposes for the prophetic word, however, were fulfilled—the announcement stimulated the repentance of an entire city's population. Like Jonah's word, Revelation as prophecy seeks mainly to stimulate faithful response among John's audience, not to provide an absolute blueprint for a fossilized future.

It might be appropriate to introduce at this juncture an important difference between John's Revelation and the book of Daniel, with which John was intimately familiar. Daniel had been instructed to "seal up" the contents of his book for a later time, the time in which the more dire "predictions" would begin to be fulfilled (Dan. 8:26; 12:4, 9). In Daniel's case, this was a means by which to account for the significant lapse of time between the lifetime of the historical Daniel (the sixth century BCE) and the denouement of the events he narrated (the crisis under Antiochus IV in the second century BCE). By contrast, John was instructed *not* to seal up the contents of his book, "for the time is near" (Rev. 22:10). This is another signal that Revelation was written for, and meant to be understood by, John's contemporaries in the late first century CE.[6] "Prophecy experts" contradict John's own perspective when they assert that twenty-first-century interpreters know what John's images signify far better than John's audiences, even though the book was *not* sealed for a later time but left open for the first-century congregations to understand.[7]

Myth #3: Revelation Is Written in a Mysterious Code

One of the most basic assertions made about Revelation is that it is written in a coded language—a code, moreover, that modern "prophecy experts" claim that we, the people of the current generation, are somehow in a better position to unlock today than the generations that have come before, including the very people to whom John addressed his book and for whom he wrote it (see myths 1 and 2). On the contrary, we are in a far less privileged position when it comes to reading Revelation, since the realities with which it interacts—the features of a landscape familiar to its first audiences—are for us a quite distant and foreign landscape. If we lived in first-century Ephesus or Pergamum, we would not have to wonder what John could be referring to when he wrote about the cult of a beast or a prostitute riding astride a seven-headed monster. And if a copy of Revelation fell into the hands of a Roman official of even modest intelligence, the subversive intent of its imagery would not be difficult to grasp in the least.

The third reading cue that John gives us is announced in the very first word of his book, *apokalypsis*, from which we get our word "apocalypse." The Greek word means "an unveiling," not "a cryptic encoding." Revelation was not sent to those seven churches as a mysterious text needing to be interpreted: It was sent to interpret the world of those readers. To put this another way, the first readers and hearers did not need a special "key" to unlock Revelation; Revelation *was* the key by which they could unlock the

6. So, rightly in regard to Rev. 22:10, Craig Koester, *Revelation*, Yale Anchor Bible (Yale University Press, 2014), 852.

7. Hal Lindsey (*There's a New World Coming*, 295) went even further: He applies the language of Daniel concerning that book's relevance for a later time (that is, its being "sealed up" for a later generation) directly to Revelation, overriding John's own claim to the contrary.

real meaning and spiritual significance of what was going on around them and so respond to it faithfully. Revelation "lifted the veil" from prominent features and persons in the landscape of these seven audiences, so that those Christians could see things in their world as they "really were" in light of the bigger picture of God's purposes for the world and the larger picture of the great and long-standing revolt against God, which God would ultimately crush.

John's apocalypse is not unique in Jewish literature. There are many such narratives of experiences of otherworldly journeys and conversations with otherworldly beings (for example, Daniel 7–12, 1 Enoch, 4 Ezra, 2 Baruch, and the Apocalypse of Abraham, to name a few). A typical feature of these apocalypses is that they open up windows on the spaces beyond normal, lived experience—for example, the activity of the throne room of God in heaven, or the Abyss or infernal regions where demons or the damned carry on their activities—as well as the times beyond the audience's contemporary situation and beyond "normal" history—for example, angelic rebellions against God in the past or God's interventions to judge and bring human society back into line with God's standards in the near or distant future. Thus apocalypses set an audience's space within the context of a larger, invisible world, and they set the audience's time in the context of a sacred history of God's activity and carefully defined plan. In so doing, they place the present moment and the challenges of the present situation in an interpretive framework, often explicitly evaluating and addressing those challenges and that situation in light of that larger backdrop derived from the sacred tradition.

Revelation spreads before the eyes of the Christians in Asia Minor that larger canopy of space and time that puts their mundane reality, along with its challenges and choices, in its "true" light and proper perspective. Their world will look different when seen in the light of the endless worship that surrounds God's throne, the reality and ferocity of God's judgments upon idolaters, and the rewards of faithfulness. Consequently, the Christian audiences' interests in and responses to their world will be changed. While Revelation may appear, then, to lift the veil from future events, Revelation's ultimate goal is to lift the veil from actors, events, and choices available to the first-century Christians John addressed.

This orientation remains quite different from a fourth interpretative approach that has been prominent in the history of interpretation—the *idealist* approach, which could also be called the "spiritual," "allegorical," or even "archetypal" reading. The idealist approach does not read Revelation as primarily a collection of predictions (like the preterist, historicist, and futurist approaches). Rather, it approaches Revelation as a text that uses symbol, vivid imagery, and dramatic action to express transcendent truths that are valid in every generation. It essentially reads Revelation for *timeless* truth, communicated symbolically, about the cosmic battle between good and evil or the trials that must be overcome by the human soul. In so doing, however, the idealist approach violates John's own perspective on the message—that it is imminent, and therefore of special *timeliness*, for the congregations to which he writes. In this way, the idealist reading also overlooks the close correlation of Revelation's primary symbols with the political and economic realities that characterized Roman Asia Minor.

To sum up: (1) As a pastoral letter, Revelation addresses that which is of concern to seven specific congregations that have grown up within the Roman province of Asia Minor in the second half of the first century. (2) As a prophetic word, Revelation announces God's perspective on the congregations' character and challenges, confirming loyalty to Christ and his covenant where such loyalty appears, rebuking unfaithfulness to the covenant where it appears, and calling for repentance. (3) As an apocalypse, Revelation sets before the audience the "bigger picture," both in terms of space and time, that illumines and interprets what the Christians see happening around them. It helps them identify the *real* challenges facing them in their situation, orienting them to respond to those challenges in a manner consonant with that "bigger picture."

Reading Revelation as a pastoral letter, early Christian prophecy, and apocalypse orients us toward Revelation in a very different way from those who read it as a road map for our future or as a countdown to the end. It orients us to a way of reading, moreover, that coheres better with how we read the rest of Scripture, a way of reading that helps us hear more of Revelation's call and challenge to us in our situation apart from the distracting conversation about determining if or when some "countdown" has begun.

This approach to Revelation summons us to immerse ourselves in the lived environment of the congregations addressed by John so that we can discover (1) what it was that he found to be objectionable in the practices around and within the churches, (2) what he found commendable or objectionable in the churches' responses to the challenges of walking in line with the lordship of God and of his Christ, and (3) what he wanted to see communities of disciples do to live even more fully in line with God's purposes and God's call to seek justice and wholeness for all people. This gives us a basis from which to discern what questions and challenges John would pose to us as communities of disciples living in the midst of our contemporary social, political, economic, and global orders. Understanding how John brought the resources of Scripture, prayer, and worship to bear on the situations of his congregations gives us direction for our own process of discernment, so that we can move closer to seeing our world from God's point of view and, therefore, to knowing how to respond to its challenges and entanglements in a way that reflects more closely our primary allegiance to the "kingdom of our Lord and of his Messiah" (Rev. 11:15).

Reflection

1. What approaches to Revelation described in this chapter have you encountered prior to this study?
2. What attracts you to one or more of these approaches?
3. What concerns or disturbs you about one or more of these approaches?
4. What strengths and what limitations do you see in the approach taken in this book?

2

Roman Asia at a Glance

Once we give recognition to the fact that Revelation is a letter addressed to seven very real communities of Christians spread throughout the Roman province of Asia in western Türkiye, we are free to read it as a piece of communication that reveals its meaning and message most fully when we immerse ourselves in the contexts and conversations of its ancient audience. As we begin to enter into the world of those Christian communities, then, what do we see? What was the everyday context of the lives of those Christians in Ephesus or Pergamum, for example, and what did they see as they walked from their apartments through the downtown spaces of their cities?[1]

A World with Deeply Held Religious Convictions

Perhaps the first and most obvious thing they would have seen was the many people who did not share their convictions about God and God's Christ. An often overlooked challenge for early Christians is the bare fact that the vast majority of people around them had little or no place for the God of Israel or his crucified Messiah. They might have acknowledged this God as a tribal deity of a particular people within Rome's empire, but certainly not as a deity as important, imposing, or relevant as the Jews had historically made their God out to be. If they acknowledged Jesus at all, it was probably as an executed revolutionary—a failure at best and a shameful criminal at worst. The lack of confirmation of the Christians' worldview in the attitudes

1. For an imaginative yet diligently researched approach to this task, see David A. deSilva, *A Week in the Life of Ephesus* (IVP Academic, 2020).

and practices of their neighbors, who lived (probably often happily) without a care for the God of Jesus the Messiah, was undoubtedly a constant invitation to question the correctness of their own convictions that enjoyed so little social reinforcement outside the small circles of Christ-followers gathering in the private spaces of the wealthier converts' houses.

Their neighbors' religious commitments were represented architecturally and spatially in the many cult sites of the traditional Greco-Roman and local gods and of the emperors, the representations of Roman imperialism. Ephesus, for example, was famous throughout the Mediterranean for its Temple of Artemis, one of the seven wonders of the ancient world, a source of great civic pride and focus of civic identity.

FIGURE 2.1. A cult statue of Diana/Artemis from the first century CE discovered buried at Ephesus. The image in the great Temple of Artemis would have closely resembled this smaller version. (Photo by author.)

Antipater of Sidon, a notable tourist in the ancient world active in the late second and early first centuries BCE, speaks of the Temple of Artemis as the crowning sight of all his travels:

> I have set eyes on the wall of lofty Babylon on which is a road for chariots, and the statue of Zeus by the Alpheus, and the hanging gardens, and the colossus of the Sun, and the huge labour of the high pyramids, and the vast tomb of Mausolus; but when I saw the house of Artemis that mounted to the clouds, those other marvels lost their brilliancy, and I said, "Lo, apart from Olympus, the Sun never looked on aught so grand." (*Greek Anthology* 9.58 LCL, Paton)

Top, FIGURE 2.2. Silver cistophorus (tetradrachm) of Claudius (emperor 41–54 CE), the reverse showing the cult statue of Diana (Artemis) standing in her celebrated temple in Ephesus. (Courtesy of Classical Numismatic Group, LLC; www.CNGcoins.com.) See page 171 for color version.

Bottom, FIGURE 2.3. Silver cistophorus of Hadrian (emperor 117–138 CE) with the cult statue of Diana (Artemis) in sharper detail on the reverse, bearing witness to the persistence of this image's importance in the province of Asia. (Courtesy of Classical Numismatic Group, LLC; www.CNGcoins.com.)

The dimensions of the Temple of Artemis were staggering. It had a footprint of 425 by 220 feet, its roof supported by 127 columns 60 feet in height (Pliny the Elder, *Natural History* 36.21.95). The temple sat a mile, more or less, from each of the city's main entrance gates. A regular calendar of festivals and processions kept the city and temple connected by streams of devotees celebrating the deity that protected Ephesus and gave it international fame.[2] Coins minted in Ephesus and inscriptions erected throughout the city draw attention daily to the city's patron goddess and her temple (see figures 2.2, 2.3). The story of Paul's visit to Ephesus in Acts 19 provides some insight into the connections between a famous temple, the tourist economy and related businesses (like the manufacturing of silver replicas of the cult statue of the

2. See Xenophon of Ephesus, *Ephesian Tale* 1.2–3, for an ancient literary representation of one such festival.

goddess as souvenirs), and civic pride, as well as the manner in which the proclamation of the Christian gospel was seen to collide with these at every level. But though prominent, Artemis was not worshiped alone. The visitor to the archaeological site of Ephesus would find temples and shrines to Cybele (the regional mother goddess) and Hestia (the goddess of the hearth), as well as the newer imperial gods (see below). Small statues of and altars to various deities bore witness to ritual devotions commonly practiced in private homes as well.

The acropolis of Roman Pergamum—another well-excavated example—was studded with prominent cultic sites of the traditional Greek divinities. A vast altar dedicated to Zeus, surrounded by columned porches and set upon a raised marble platform approached by twenty-eight steps, crowned the southern crest of the hill, overlooking all the territory below. It covered a footprint of 120 by 110 feet and rose to a height of 40 feet. Its porticoes were adorned with statues of a wide variety of deities, whose collective battle against and defeat of the giants was also celebrated in a larger-than-life frieze decorating the perimeter of the structure.

FIGURE 2.4. The Acropolis of Pergamum. The white, columned ruins of the Temple of Trajan dominate the upper left. The site of the monumental Altar of Zeus is just out of the frame in the upper right. A temple of Athena originally stood above the theater. The ruins of the Temple of Dionysus are visible halfway down the hill from Trajan's Temple. (Photo by author.) See page 165 for color version.

FIGURE 2.5. Friedrich Thiersch's 1882 reconstruction of the Acropolis of Pergamum in the second century CE (Antikensammlung, Staatliche Museen zu Berlin). The Altar of Zeus is in the foreground, the precincts of the Temple of Athena above, center, and the Temple of Trajan in the background. See page 165 for color version.

FIGURE 2.6. The site of the Altar of Zeus, overlooking Pergamum/Bergama. The prominent location of this altar on the brow of the acropolis recommends it as the local monument referred to as "Satan's throne" in the oracle to the Christians in Pergamum. (Photo by author.) See page 166 for color version.

FIGURE 2.7. The monumental Altar of Zeus as reconstructed in the Pergamon Museum, Berlin. The carved reliefs surrounding the structure depict scenes from the mythic battle of the Olympian gods against the giants. (Courtesy of Wikipedia Commons; photo by Jan Mehlich.) See page 166 for color version.

On the plateau just above it stood a temple to Athena, a structure with a footprint of 70 by 40 feet surrounded by a large colonnaded courtyard. The complex overlooked a vast theater carved into the steep hillside. At stage level, about halfway down the height of the acropolis, a temple to Dionysus stood in close proximity to the theater, whose productions were often connected with the worship of that god. On the southwest slope of the acropolis sat a temple and precinct sacred to Demeter, with the customary altar before the temple and with distinctive stadium seating running along one of its longer sides.

At a lower level, in close proximity to the gymnasium, stood a temple to Hera, the queen of the gods, and a shrine to Hermes and Heracles, deities representing swiftness and strength and, therefore, typically associated with the activities of the gymnasium. About a mile to the southwest of the acropolis—and connected to it by a "sacred road"—was a sprawling complex called an *Asklepion*, a kind of health spa where people with various ailments would seek prescriptions for healing from Asklepios, the god of healing, in their dreams. Literary witnesses and somewhat more limited archaeological work have allowed similar catalogs to be made for Smyrna, Sardis, and Laodicea. (Thyatira and Philadelphia would also no doubt have had cult sites for the traditional gods, but archaeological work is severely restricted in those cities.)

Top, FIGURE 2.8. Temple of Demeter, Pergamum. (Photo by author.)

Bottom, FIGURE 2.9. Cult scene, Temple of Demeter. A small part of a carved relief that decorated the altar of the Temple of Demeter on the Pergamum acropolis. A priestess, holding a libation bowl, stands between the sacrificial animal and the sacred fire on the altar. (Photo by author.)

Alongside temples to the traditional gods stood temples and other sacred cult sites dedicated to the goddess Roma, the deified personification of the city at the heart of the empire, and to various emperors themselves. Thus, one would find in Ephesus a double shrine to Julius Caesar and Artemis behind the north portico of the civic agora—the administrative forum—of the city. The central courtyard of the administrative forum also became the sacred precinct of a freestanding temple to Augustus and Roma in the late first century BCE. Toward the end of the first century CE, a magnificent temple was built in honor of Domitian and his family, the Flavian household, upon an artificially extended plateau, dominating upper Ephesus.

Smyrna erected its first temple to Roma as early as 195 BCE, long before it was popular to do so in Asia Minor. By the time of Revelation, locals would also see a grand temple to Tiberius, his mother Livia, and the Roman

FIGURE 2.10. Temple of Julius Caesar and Artemis, Ephesus. The twin shrines once stood atop the stairway on the left side of the picture; the courtyard, once surrounded by columns on its other three sides, is center frame. (Photo by author.) See page 167 for color version.

Top, FIGURE 2.11. The Plateau of the Temple of Domitian (the Flavian Temple) in Ephesus. The Flavian Temple originally stood over the flat, grassy space above the arches that formed part of its foundation. From this place, it dominated the civic spaces of Ephesus. (Photo by author.)

Bottom, FIGURE 2.12. Remains of altar from the Temple of Domitian. The short side is decorated with a bull, tied and ready for sacrifice; the longer side features pieces of armor and weapons, commemorating the emperor's conquests. (Photo by author.) See page 167 for color version.

Senate built in Smyrna. In Pergamum, a temple was built to honor Roma and Augustus as early as 19 BCE (with construction starting a decade earlier). An even more impressive temple complex would be built atop the acropolis in the early second century to honor Trajan. Laodicea also boasted a temple to Domitian and his wife, Domitia, by the late first century.

Left two, FIGURE 2.13. A denarius of Augustus (emperor 31 BCE–14 CE), showing Pergamum's Temple to Rome and Augustus, completed in 19 BCE, on the reverse. The legend *Com Asiae* is an abbreviation for *Communitas Asiae,* the provincial council of Asia responsible for, among other things, the promotion of the imperial cult. (Courtesy of Numismatica Ars Classica AG; auction 64, lot 1038.)

Right two, FIGURE 2.14. Silver tetradrachm minted in Asia during the reign of Claudius (emperor 41–54 CE), showing the cult images of Augustus and the goddess Roma inside their temple. Roma is reaching out her hand to place a victory wreath on Augustus's head. (Courtesy of Numismatica Ars Classica AG; auction 64, lot 2482.)

The sight of these temples and the activity that made them burst into life on holidays throughout the year would remain an ever-present invitation to John's congregations to remember another story—the public story—about the nature of Roman rule. According to John, this public story that constantly surrounded his congregations was incompatible with God's perspective on Roman rule. As this is a critical element of Revelation's word to the churches, we will give it detailed attention in the next chapter. For now, what is most important to recognize is the fact that early Christians were challenged to hold onto a distinctly minority view in the midst of a population that oriented itself around the traditional Greco-Roman gods and that located itself within the story of Roman rule as a manifestation of the gods' provision for humanity's well-being.

The significance of this never impressed itself upon me until I spent two months in Sri Lanka, where Christians account for only 7–8 percent of a deeply religious population. Almost 70 percent would claim to adhere to Buddhism, with perhaps 15–16 percent following Hinduism, and another 7 or

8 percent following Islam. For the converts or children of converts to Christianity in that setting, the prominence and pervasiveness of Buddhist statues and shrines, together with the visible signs of devotion to the Buddha—from activity at those shrines to the weaving and purchase of flower garlands for offerings sold in the marketplace alongside shops that sell bread, fruit, and cell phone minutes—serve as a constant reminder of their own or their family's departure from the worldview and story held to be true by the vocal majority of their neighbors.

A World of Economic Opportunity

Christians moving from their apartments into the public spaces of Ephesus would have also seen everywhere the signs of trade and flourishing economic markets, not least of all in the bustling commercial forums of these cities. The harbor at Ephesus, now silted up after centuries of neglect, was once a major port in the eastern Mediterranean with a constant flow of merchandise coming along trade routes from the north and the east to be shipped out to ports closer to the center of the world, and above all to Rome itself. This offered the urban Ephesian, and residents of other major cities tied into the network of trade in the province, many opportunities to plug into the local economy or the transportation industry, thus securing one's slice of the Roman pie. The inscription above the entrance to a mausoleum just outside the northern gate of Hierapolis, a city not ten miles away from Laodicea, celebrates one such ship captain, who boasts that he made seventy-two trips around the southern cape of Greece bearing goods to Italy from Roman Asia. The size of the mausoleum testifies to the money to be made from such activity.

Christians in any of these thriving cities would have seen many families living normal, perhaps even better-than-average lives, and thus would have seen much that was desirable for themselves and their own families. The prosperity promised by Rome, and the possibility of sharing this prosperity, was a particularly important aspect of the situation of these congregations. The lure of wealth had sunk its hooks quite deep, for example, into the mouths of Laodicean Christians, who could boast of their own prosperity as participants in their local economy while failing to recognize their deep poverty in Christ's eyes, as John sees it. No doubt the hope for economic prosperity also provided the main motivation for developing a theology that could accommodate "eating food sacrificed to idols," something John identifies as a feature of the message of rival prophets active among the Christians in Pergamum and Thyatira (and rebuffed in Ephesus).

Above, FIGURE 2.15. Roman street leading to the original harbor of Ephesus. The ancient Ephesus harbor is now little more than a swamp because of centuries of silting. In ancient times, this harbor gave Ephesus direct access to the Aegean Sea and made it a major center for trade and commerce in the Mediterranean. (Photo by author.)

Right above, FIGURE 2.16. The mausoleum of Flavius Zeuxis and his family in Hierapolis.

Right below, FIGURE 2.17. The inscription above the doorway to Flavius Zeuxis's mausoleum.

Suspicions Concerning Christians' Loyalties

Another important question to ask if we are to enter into the context of the recipients of Revelation and understand the challenges that they faced and that John addresses is, What would the Christians' neighbors have seen when they looked at the Christians in their midst? They would have seen Christians, ironically perhaps, as "atheists"—people who failed to acknowledge the existence of the gods of their neighbors and, in the majority of cases, the gods of their own forebears. Here in their midst was a group of people who used to give the gods their due but who now had turned their backs upon proper piety, both in public and in private, and who spoke of their neighbors' and families' gods as sticks and stones. Christians, like the members of other groups nurtured within Judaism, did not merely devote themselves to a particular deity but also claimed that no other deity existed alongside the One. Such a position was labeled "impiety" (Aelius Aristides, *Or.* 46.309) or "atheism," the specific charge on which the emperor Domitian executed or banished several high-ranking Roman converts to Judaism (Dio Cassius, *Hist.* 67.14.1–3).

The Christians' neighbors, who depended upon the stability now maintained by the empire, saw potential enemies of the Roman peace. Christians were, after all, followers of a man whom a Roman procurator had duly executed for sedition. A central focus in the proclamation of their leaders was some future day when this executed leader would return to bring Roman power to an end in favor of some "kingdom of God," an upheaval that would not be welcomed by (or favorable to) the majority. In short, they would see formerly decent citizens or children of decent citizens who had gotten into some very bad company by being lured into this foreign superstition.

Pressures Reflected in the Seven Oracles

In this setting of opportunity and tension, of trying to hold onto the Christian hope without letting go of too much of this world's promise, what pressures would we find Christians experiencing? Here Revelation is, as a pastoral word to these believers, our primary evidence for these pressures, since John, giving voice to the various diagnoses of the glorified Jesus, explicitly brings these pressures to expression. Other New Testament texts, however, also bear witness that these same pressures were widely experienced by Christians throughout the eastern Roman Empire in some form or other.

First, they no doubt felt the drive within themselves to enjoy the elements of "the good life" that were readily available to their neighbors and that they formerly enjoyed themselves without scruple. There was doubtless the ongoing urge to blend in and thus to drink in the benefits of participating in their city's life and economy. This would have required some level of integration into the religious practice of their city and their associates—that is, into the acknowledgment of idols and worship of the traditional gods. There were local preachers and prophets in Pergamum and Thyatira who sought to help make this work for them theologically, so that they could hold on to Christ and live prosperous (or at least financially secure) lives at the same time.

> You have some there holding to the teaching of Balaam, who taught Balak to cast a stumbling block before the children of Israel, so that they would eat food sacrificed to idols and practice fornication. (Rev. 2:14 AT)
>
> I have this against you: you allow that woman Jezebel, who calls herself a prophetess and is teaching and leading my servants astray so that they practice fornication and eat food sacrificed to idols. (2:20 AT)

Christians in some communities felt the pressure brought down upon them by local synagogues, whose members had never been thrilled with this Jewish heresy that seemed to spring up everywhere, and who had every reason to publicly distance themselves from anything with a revolutionary flavor since the dismal failure of the First Jewish Revolt.

> I know your affliction. . . . I know the slander on the part of those who say that they are Jews and are not but are a synagogue of Satan. (2:9)
>
> I will make those of the synagogue of Satan who say that they are Jews and are not but are lying—I will make them come and bow down before your feet, and they will learn that I have loved you. (3:9)

Many felt pressure from their neighbors, who did not approve of the facets of the Christians' witness and practice that called into question their much-beloved realities—particularly the existence and favor of the gods and the promise of endless peace and prosperity under Roman rule. These locals even went so far as to lynch a Christian named Antipas in Pergamum—and John's audiences would all remember from reports told about Nero's Rome what happened to Christians when the beast really rears its ugly heads.[3]

> I also know that you are enduring patiently and bearing up for the sake of my name and that you have not grown weary. (2:3)
>
> You did not deny your faith in me even in the days of Antipas my witness, my faithful one, who was killed among you, where Satan lives. (2:13)

But John is also particularly interested in the complete lack of pressure that some believers encountered or, perhaps better, the fact that some believers encountered exactly and only the same pressures that their non-Christian neighbors encountered, because their lives were no different. The Christians in Sardis and Laodicea seem to pose a serious problem for John precisely because they were so untroubled by what was going on around them and had become so much a part of it.

> I know your works; you have a reputation that you are alive, but you are dead. . . . I have not found your works completed in the sight of my God. . . . Yet you have a few persons in Sardis who have not soiled their clothes. (3:1–4 AT)
>
> You say, "I am rich, I have prospered, and I need nothing," and you do not know that you are wretched, pitiable, poor, blind, and naked. (3:17 AT)

John addresses all of these realities in Revelation, and not merely on their own terms but under a particular lens—the lens of the larger story, the sacred story, of which they are a part. This story needed such strong reinforcement that John addresses his readers not just with a pastoral letter, nor just with prophetic oracles, but with an apocalypse—a revelation of the truth of that larger story.

3. We do not have any sure knowledge of the circumstances of Antipas's death, whether it was the result of an official trial and sentence or an unauthorized murder (which, given the unpopularity of the Christian movement, would plausibly have prompted no investigations, let alone convictions).

3

Divine Emperor, Eternal Rome: The Public Story About Roman Imperialism

THE MEMBERS OF THE CHURCHES JOHN ADDRESSES WERE EXPOSED TO TWO very different stories about the "way things are," the "way the world works," and therefore "the way to get along" to their advantage. Inscriptions throughout the cities, the coins with which all business was transacted, statues, temples, civic processions, public announcements—all the available media of the first century—told the first, public story and kept its picture of the "way things are" visible. John tells a very different story, drawing a very different picture—the view from the throne of God and the Lamb. He does this in order to motivate the Christ-followers in these cities to resolve the challenges they faced in the way that nurtures a clear, uncompromising witness to that God and his Anointed. Here we will explore the public story in depth, for it is the story foundational to the society and structures in which the members of the seven churches live, and the story that John most directly challenges in his revelation of the way things really are in the sight of the one God.

The Official Narrative About Rome

The public story of Rome began with the fall of Troy, from whose ashes emerged a hero, Aeneas, who would travel to Italy with a band of Troy's survivors and plant the seeds of a world empire. Julius Caesar would trace his family line back to Aeneas through his son Ascanius—also known as Iulus—and thus also claim descent from the goddess Venus (Aphrodite), Aeneas's divine mother. Aeneas's story was told by Virgil, a poet in Augustus's court and author of the *Aeneid*, the court epic of the Augustan age. Virgil celebrated the promise of Zeus, the king of the gods, that the Romans, who would spring from Aeneas's line, would "rule the sea and all the lands about it" (*Aen.* 1.236–37). Virgil referred here to the *orbis terrarum*, the "circle of the lands" about the Mediterranean that was considered the civilized world. The map developed under the direction of Marcus Vipsanius Agrippa, Augustus's right-hand man during his war against Marc Antony and his consolidation of power, illustrates this concept. The Mediterranean Sea stands at the center of the map, with all the known territories of Europe, Africa, and Asia (as far as India and Sri Lanka) arranged around the Mediterranean in a great

FIGURE 3.1. Marcus Agrippa's map of the world. This modern reconstruction of Agrippa's map from 20 CE (known only through descriptions) well illustrates why the inhabited world was spoken of as the *orbis terrarum*, the "circle of lands." (Courtesy of www.cartographic-images.net.)

circle with a small opening between Spain and North Africa (the Straits of Gibraltar).[1]

This was the "world" that counted. Zeus asserted that the destiny of Rome would be to "bring the whole world under law's dominion" (*Aen.* 4.232). Indeed, as the wings of the Roman eagle overshadowed more and more of the Mediterranean basin, it was commonly credited with *universal* rule and seen by many to exercise "authority over every tribe and people and language and nation" (Rev. 13:7). Minucius Felix, a second-century Christian, wrote of the Romans that "their power and authority has occupied the circuit of the whole world," referring once again to the concept of the *orbis terrarum*. "Thus it has propagated its empire beyond the paths of the sun and the bounds of the ocean itself" (*Octavius* 6). Rome would thus have been readily identified as "the great city that rules over the kings of the earth" (Rev. 17:18). These writers were aware that other nations existed that were not under Roman dominion—at least, not yet—and that indeed sometimes posed a threat to Rome's dominion in some areas and to Rome's borders. Nevertheless, "authority over the kings of the earth" and over "the whole world" was regularly attributed to Rome during this period.

Plutarch, a near-contemporary of John, celebrated the rise of Rome and its success in uniting the Mediterranean region (though he, too, notably uses the language of "the world" rather than just a portion of it): "Rome developed and grew strong, and attached to herself not only nations and peoples but foreign kingdoms beyond the sea; and then at last the world found stability and security, when the controlling power entered into a single, unwavering cycle and world order of peace" ("On the Fortune of the Romans" 2 [*Moralia* 317] LCL, Babbitt). The gifts and graces of Rome were, according to Virgil, "To pacify, to impose the rule of law, to spare the conquered, battle down the proud" (*Aen.* 6.851–53).[2]

The power of Rome was visually portrayed in the image of the goddess Roma, the visible representation of the "order," the "rule of law," the "peace" and "stability" that Rome's imperial rule brought. She was often featured on the reverse of coins; she is more prominently visible in the cult statues throughout the Mediterranean. Roma was given the epithet *Aeterna*, an

1. While no copies of the map itself have survived, it appears to have been the basis for the description of the world found in Pliny, *Natural History* 6.39, written before 69 CE.

2. Virgil, *The Aeneid*, trans. Robert Fitzgerald (Random House, 1981), 190.

epithet that persists to this day when we hear Rome called "the Eternal City." Thus Rome's supporters and propagandists advanced the bold claim that Rome's destiny was unchanging and everlasting. Plutarch reflected this when he affirmed that Rome provided a "secure mooring cable" for the world and used adjectives such as "unwavering" to describe her rule, forgetting all the lessons of world history. "Prophecy experts" insist on looking still to *our* future for a beast and his "one-world empire" because they have not looked closely at the images projected of Rome in the first century and at the perception of the Roman Empire held by most of its inhabitants (including John and his audience) and purposefully promoted by imperial propaganda.

Top, FIGURE 3.2. Sesterce of Nero (emperor 54–68 CE). The reverse features the goddess Roma seated, holding a representation of victory (the goddess Nikē) in her right hand. (Courtesy of Classical Numismatic Group, LLC; www.CNGcoins.com.)

Bottom, FIGURE 3.3. Aureus of Hadrian (emperor 117–138 CE), featuring the goddess Roma, seated, holding "Victory" in her extended arm. The legend reads *Roma Aeterna,* "Eternal Rome." (Courtesy of Classical Numismatic Group, LLC; www.CNGcoins.com.)

FIGURE 3.4. Denarius of Trajan (emperor 98–117 CE). The reverse shows the personification of "the Providence of the Augusti," the divine principle that gives stability (signified by the pillar on which Providence rests) to the whole world (the globe at her feet). (Courtesy of Classical Numismatic Group, LLC; www.CNGcoins.com.)

Rome was also celebrated as the source of prosperity for the whole world. The luxury of Rome was taken as a sign that a golden age of prosperity had returned to the entire Mediterranean. In a speech praising Rome, Aelius Aristides, a younger contemporary of John, described the scene in Rome thus:

> Around lie the continents far and wide, pouring an endless flow of goods to Rome. There is brought from every land and sea whatever is brought forth by the seasons and is produced by all countries, rivers, lakes, and the skills of Greeks and foreigners. Anyone who wants to behold all these products must either journey through the whole world to see them or else come to this city. One can see so many cargoes from India or if you wish from Arabia . . . that one may surmise that the trees there have been left permanently bare, and that those people must come here whenever they need anything! (*To Rome* 11–13)[3]

Aristides seemed to be oblivious to the obvious downside of the Roman economy, but he was a member of the elite and hence a voice for the public, official story of Rome. Such elite sources painted a picture of a world power that brought tremendous benefits to humankind: an end to civil strife, protection from invasion, improvement of means of travel by land (through expert road construction) and by sea (through expansion of ports and harbors), as well as the dramatic reduction of brigandage and piracy. Trade was facilitated, the steady distribution of grain and relief in times of shortfall improved, and the rule of law maintained. Much of this is true. Moreover, individual emperors

3. Naphtali Lewis and Meyer Reinhold, eds., *Roman Civilization: Selected Readings, vol. 2, The Empire* (Columbia University Press, 1990), 123.

gave significant benefits to cities in Asia Minor, reinforcing the "public discourse" with tangible demonstrations of its truth. Tiberius provided financial assistance to rebuild several cities in Asia Minor after an earthquake in 17 CE, including Sardis and Philadelphia. Nero dredged the harbor of Ephesus, restoring the city's most important economic asset. Domitian provided Laodicea with a stadium and Smyrna with an aqueduct. Rome could be a great safety net and a source of significant blessings.

FIGURE 3.5. The base of a statue erected in honor of Tiberius by the fourteen cities in Roman Asia affected by the earthquake of 17 CE and rebuilt with the help of imperial funding. The visible side features representations of the patron gods of Sardis (left) and Magnesia (right). (Photo courtesy of Olga Lyubimova.)

According to this public story, Divine Providence was at work in the rise and reign of Rome, and it was particularly at work in the rise and reign of Augustus and his successors. Rome was an empire long before Augustus, in the sense that the Roman Republic already controlled most of the lands around the Mediterranean. But the Republic offered power-hungry senators (like Marcus Licinius Crassus, Sextus Pompeius, and Julius Caesar) too much opportunity for factionalism and, ultimately, civil war. The Mediterranean was twice subjected to all the horrors of civil war prior to 31 BCE, when

Octavian, soon to be given the name "Augustus" ("revered one"), finally emerged from the strife victorious. He quickly forgave the armies of his rival, Marc Antony, uniting their power to his own.

"By universal consent," Augustus accepted perpetual powers in the republic. Thus government became stable and the provinces flourished again. The phrase "by universal consent" was a vital element of promoting Augustus's rule as legitimate in the early empire. Toward the end of his life, Augustus drew up a list of his political and military actions and achievements on behalf of the Roman order—the *Res Gestae Augusti* (referred to as the *Res Gestae Divi Augusti* after his posthumous deification). After his death, this list was inscribed in public spaces across the empire, reminding people everywhere of the legitimacy of the new order ushered in by Augustus and continued by his successor, Tiberius.[4] In this list, he notes "having obtained all things by universal consent" and being given the title "'Augustus' by universal decree." Far from being a tyrant, this inscription claims, Augustus had greatness thrust upon him by universal acclaim, and appropriately so, given all he had done on behalf of the world.

Reinforcing the Public Story

A particularly important expression for naming Augustus's greatest gift and for summing up all of his gifts was the *Pax Augusta*, the "Augustan Peace" or "Peace of Augustus." This was the beginning of the "Roman peace" (*Pax Romana*), to which reference would be made throughout the imperial period. It celebrated the end of the series of civil wars, as well as the new ordering of the government throughout the provinces of the empire. The senate commemorated this in an extraordinary way. As Augustus relates in his own words,

> When I returned to Rome from Spain and Gaul [that is, in 13 BCE], having settled affairs successfully in these provinces, . . . the senate decreed that an altar of Augustan Peace should be consecrated in thanks for my return on the field

4. The text was inscribed on bronze plates in front of Augustus's mausoleum in Rome. The best-preserved copy of the inscription was found on the Temple of Augustus and Roma in Ancyra (modern Ankara, Türkiye). Fragments were recovered from the monumental entrance to the sacred precinct of the Temple of Augustus and Roma in Pisidian Antioch, as well as in Apollonia, both also in modern Türkiye.

> of Mars, and ordered magistrates and priests and Vestal Virgins to perform an annual sacrifice there. (*Res Gestae Divi Augusti* 12.2)[5]

This altar, which has been uncovered and fully restored, is housed within a marble monument of about forty feet square, into which is built a staircase leading up to the altar proper. It sat in a prominent location on the Flaminian Way, a major road running through Rome. This monument was given empire-wide notice through display on the reverse of several coin mintings. This is just one manifestation of the empire's acclamation of Augustus as the bringer of peace and, with it, the promise of a new era.

FIGURE 3.6. The Altar of the Augustan Peace, Rome. (Photo by author.)

An inscription found at Priene, another city in Asia Minor about twenty miles south of Ephesus, similarly captures the spirit of this new age. In 9 BCE, the provincial council (the *Koinon Asias*), which was the regional body entrusted with various duties including the promotion of "the imperial cult," announced a contest for the best proposal for the most appropriate way to

5. Alison E. Cooley, *Res Gestae Divi Augusti: Text, Translation, and Commentary* (Cambridge University Press, 2009), 70.

FIGURE 3.7. Bronze *as* (or *assarion*, 1/16 of a denarius) of Nero (emperor 54–68 CE). The "Altar of Peace" erected by Augustus adorns the reverse. (Courtesy of Classical Numismatic Group, LLC; www.CNGcoins.com.)

honor Augustus. The winning proposal came from Paullus Fabius Maximus, the proconsul of Asia for that year. On his recommendation, the council issued a decree that the birthday of Augustus would become the official "New Year's Day" of the calendar year:

> Whereas Providence that orders all our lives has, in her display of concern and generosity in our behalf, adorned our lives with the highest good: Augustus, whom she has filled with virtue for the benefit of humanity, . . . who has made war to cease and who shall put everything in . . . order, . . . with the result that the birthday of our god signaled the beginning of Good News (*euangeliōn*) for the world because of him; . . . the Greeks in Asia decreed that the New Year begin for all the cities on September 23, which is the birthday of Augustus.[6]

Speaking of a divine figure's birth ("the birthday of our god") as the "beginning of the good news" for the world should cause readers of the New Testament to take notice.[7] The word from the inscription translated as "good news" here is a form of *euangelion*, the same Greek word that is so prominent in the New Testament (whether translated as "good news" or "gospel"). This inscription lauded Augustus as Providence's provision for the "highest good" of the people, a ruler whom Providence "filled with excellence for the benefit

6. Translation from Frederick W. Danker, *Benefactor: Epigraphic Study of a Graeco-Roman and New Testament Semantic Field* (Clayton, 1982), 217, with minor modifications for clarity.

7. When Luke speaks of the birth of Jesus as the "good news" concerning the appearing of a "Savior" who will benefit "all the people" (Luke 2:10–11)—a story in which Augustus appears offstage merely as the person drawing up a list to make sure he can get everyone's money—his readers would have understood the political implications of his proclamation of Jesus's place in the divine scheme of things.

of humanity." The text of this resolution was inscribed in temples to Augustus across the province of Asia, making its language available to the citizens of the seven cities. Similar acclamations of the reigning emperor reverberate to the very end of the first century CE. Concerning Domitian, Statius writes: "Lo! A god is he! At Jupiter's command he rules for him the happy world" (*Silvae* 4.3.128–29 LCL, Mozley, adapted). Inscriptions found throughout the eastern empire—from Athens to Smyrna to Gerasa—laud emperors from Augustus through Hadrian as "savior" (*sōtēr*). By the standards of Christian language, acclamations of the emperor were no less than messianic.

FIGURE 3.8. A nearly life-size carved relief showing Claudius (Augustus?) as lord of earth and sea. The emperor stands with one foot on land and one on the sea. The personified earth offers him a cornucopia (the fruit of the land), while the personified sea offers him a rudder (a symbol of navigation and trade). This is one of almost a hundred reliefs that once decorated the processional way leading to the Temple of Augustus and Roma in Aphrodisias, a city in Roman Asia. (Photo by author.)

Temples were erected first to Julius Caesar and then to Augustus across the eastern Mediterranean, where people were accustomed to treating their rulers and exceptional benefactors as gods. Nicolaus of Damascus, once a tutor in the palace of Cleopatra and later a friend of Herod the Great, explained the phenomenon in the opening of his *Life of Augustus* thus:

> Because mankind addressed him thus [as Augustus] in accordance with their estimation of his honor, they revere him with temples and sacrifices over islands and continents, organized in cities and provinces, matching the greatness of his virtue and repaying his benefactions towards them.[8]

Since the emperor's gifts were of such a magnitude that they seemed to match those sought from the traditional gods, it was deemed only fitting that the expressions of the gratitude and loyalty of his subjects should take on the forms used to communicate with the gods themselves.

Roman power was represented in the seven cities named by John in many ways, but perhaps the most prominent and enduring was the imperial cult: the temples, shrines, altars, and cult images dedicated to Augustus and to the members of his household, including those who succeeded to the imperial office. There were many such local cult temples and sites among the seven cities addressed by Revelation. Ephesus built a sizable temple to Augustus and *Dea Roma* (the goddess Roma) in the broad open courtyard of its administrative forum. With a footprint of 72 by 50 feet, it dominated the space. Ephesus also had a smaller shrine to Julius Caesar, shared with Artemis. Smyrna dedicated a temple to Roma in 195 BCE—long before it was popular to do so and at a time when Rome's influence in the region was still contested. Laodicea erected a temple to Domitian and his wife, Domitia, sometime after 81 CE.

But temples were also awarded and built at the higher and more prestigious level of the "provincial" cult of the emperors, and it is particularly with reference to the competitions for such awards that the connection between the imperial cult and civic pride made itself known in the late first and early second centuries CE. Augustus awarded Pergamum in Roman Asia and Nicomedia in the neighboring province of Bithynia the honor of hosting provincial temples built to him and to *Dea Roma* in 29 BCE, for which these cities were granted the honorific title *neōkoros*—"temple warden" or "temple keeper." This elevated Pergamum above its peer cities in the province of Asia

8. S. R. F. Price, *Rituals and Power: The Roman Imperial Cult in Asia Minor* (Cambridge, 1984), 1.

FIGURE 3.9. The archaeological footprint of the Temple of Augustus and Roma in Ephesus.

FIGURE 3.10. The well-preserved Temple of Augustus and Roma ("Maison Carrée") in Nîmes, France. The temple in Ephesus would have closely resembled a somewhat smaller version of this temple, also erected toward the end of the first century BCE. (Photo courtesy of Carole Raddato.)

for the remainder of Augustus's reign (as it did also, incidentally, for Nicomedia in its own province). In 26 CE, a little more than a decade into the reign of Tiberius, eleven cities in Roman Asia competed for the honor of hosting a provincial temple to Augustus's successor. By a process of elimination, the competition came down to Smyrna and Sardis, with the Roman Senate deciding in favor of the former. Smyrna thus became *neōkoros* of the Temple of Tiberius, Livia (his mother), and the Senate. The two provincial temples in Pergamum and Smyrna are known only from the coins that celebrate them (see figs. 2.13 and 2.14 above, and 3.11). It is likely that another of the cities in Asia would have been awarded the same honor for a temple to Claudius, though no traces of this remain in the literary or archaeological evidence.

FIGURE 3.11. A bronze coin minted in Smyrna showing the provincial Temple of Tiberius, with the cult statue of the emperor wearing a toga visible in the interior. Busts of Livia and a young man personifying the Roman Senate appear on the other face of the coin. (Courtesy of Classical Numismatic Group, LLC; www.CNGcoins.com.)

Augustus's line (the "Julio-Claudian dynasty") remained strong for a century (31 BCE–68 CE), but it came to a crashing end when Nero committed suicide in 68 CE without leaving a viable heir. The empire reverted once more to chaos in the midst of civil war. The year 68–69 CE is remembered as "the year of the four emperors," each of the first three contenders (Galba, Otho, and Vitellius) enjoying their overlapping "reigns" for just a few months each. The armies of the various contenders swept across the Mediterranean from Spain to Egypt like hordes of locusts, wreaking havoc in multiple battle sites—including the capital city itself. This was also the period in which Judea and Jerusalem had been under siege with the suppression of the First Jewish Revolt against Rome. When the fourth contender, Flavius Vespasianus, emerged as the last man standing at the end of this year, everyone was prepared to embrace him, along with his two sons, as the ruler of the world. The mortal wound that threatened to dissolve the empire had found healing at last. Rome was able to stand upright once more. The cities of Asia Minor had displayed uncommon enthusiasm for the cult of the emperors since Augustus, and this enthusiasm was dramatically renewed.

FIGURE 3.12. Sesterce of Vespasian (emperor 69–79 CE) with reverse depicting Rome being lifted up from the ground (*Roma Resurges*) after the conclusion of the yearlong civil war that brought it to its knees. (Courtesy of Numismatica Ars Classica AG; auction 25, lot 410.)

Ephesus seized the opportunity to distinguish itself in the race for provincial imperial temples. It was awarded the honor of hosting the provincial Temple of Domitian (later to be rededicated to Vespasian after the Roman Senate condemned Domitian's memory). The city selected a plateau overlooking the administrative forum, artificially extending it with vaulted brick substructures to accommodate its grand visions for the complex. The temple would have a footprint of 110 by 80 feet in the midst of a colonnaded courtyard of 280 by 210 feet. It would house colossal statues of the members of the Flavian dynasty. The scale of the recovered arm and head of one statue—whether a representation of Titus or Domitian remains a matter of dispute—suggests that the cult image originally stood 24 feet tall, presenting the emperor as the larger-than-life figure he was believed to be. Having gained the honor of being a *neōkoros* city alongside Pergamum and Smyrna, the Ephesians took the novel step of incorporating this title into the city's self-identification in inscription after inscription. These would name Ephesus henceforth as "the council and the citizenry of the *neōkoros* city of the Ephesians."

Above, FIGURE 3.13. The once grand staircase giving access to the sacred precinct of the Domitian temple. The staircase was originally an interior structure, fronted by a three-story facade sporting figures carved into its columns, two of which are still visible (top left). Scholars are divided concerning whether these were an array of deities or representatives of provinces and peoples taken into the empire. (Photo by author.)

Left, FIGURE 3.14. Remains of the colossal statue of Domitian (Titus?) from the Flavian temple in Ephesus. (Photo by author.) See page 168 for color versions of both photos.

The Pergamenes, of course, were not to be outdone. They still claimed preeminence by virtue of having been the first city granted a neokorate and began describing their city thus in inscriptions: "The council and citizenry of the *first*-to-be-named-*neōkoros* city of the Pergamenes." In the early years of the second century, Pergamum would win the honor of building a massive temple to house the provincial cult of the emperor Trajan (98–117 CE), co-dedicated to Zeus, for which they were awarded the title *neōkoros* a second time. They celebrated their elevated civic identity as "the council and citizenry of the *twice*-to-be-named-*neōkoros* city of

Above, FIGURE 3.15. Part of the marble lintel that originally stood atop the Fountain of Trajan in Ephesus. The inscription reads, *[Hē N]eōkoros Ephesiōn Polis,* "The Temple-Warden City of the Ephesians." (Photo by author.)

Below, FIGURE 3.16. Detail of an inscription in the gymnasium in Pergamum, honoring the director of the facility. The Pergamenes describe themselves here as "the first to be awarded the temple wardenship" of the imperial cult in the province of Asia. (Photo by author.)

the Pergamenes" in their inscriptions. Smyrna was granted a second provincial temple during the reign of Hadrian, Trajan's successor, and thus also became a *dis neōkoros*, a "twice temple-warden" city. Hadrian would take the unprecedented step of awarding a second provincial temple in his honor to Ephesus, which thus also began to advertise itself in inscriptions as "the council and citizenry of the *twice*-to-be-named-*neōkoros* city of the Ephesians."[9] Pergamum's response? They began to describe themselves in

9. The temple to Hadrian is not the small, beautifully preserved shrine shown to tourists on the main thoroughfare of the archaeological site of Ephesus, but a massive and largely unexcavated

inscriptions as "the council and citizenry of the *first*-to-be-twice-named-*neōkoros* city of the Pergamenes"!

The cities of Asia Minor were as enthusiastic and as invested in hosting the imperial cult as modern cities are about convincing a major football team to relocate to their city or winning the bid to host the Olympics. This tells us something else about the cult of the emperors. This cult was not imposed on the provinces by the emperors; it was locally motivated, the response of provincial populations to the tremendous power of the emperor, which was perceived as truly godlike, and to the benefits that the rule of the emperor brought to the provinces. Such displays of loyalty and gratitude ensured both that the empire would remain strong (hence averting the disasters of civil war and foreign invasion and ensuring continued peace and prosperity) and that the emperor would remain well disposed toward the province (and above all, to particular cities) when imperial aid was needed. It was a most politic decision that the province's ambassadors to the emperor should also be those elites who held priesthoods in the imperial cult. The beneficent god in the temple was the face of the emperor that Rome was happy to have the provinces see. The devoted and grateful functionaries presiding in those temples were the face of the province that Asia Minor wanted Rome to see.

The imperial cult was embedded in the cults of the traditional Greco-Roman gods. Frequently, the statues of the emperor and the Olympian gods shared the same sacred space, emphasizing their connectedness. In Ephesus, for example, we find Julius and Artemis worshiped in the same temple, with a portion of the great Artemision also dedicated to Augustus. In Pergamum, the Temple of Trajan and Zeus Philios ("the Friendly") sits in close proximity to the Temple of Athena and the great altar of Zeus, and overlooks the Temple of Dionysus beside the theater, where tragedies were performed as part of festivals honoring that god. The emperor was not simply a god but also the vessel by which the traditional gods established order and showered their gifts upon humanity. As the chief priest of the Roman world (*Pontifex Maximus*), the emperor stood as mediator between the gods and the human race. Many coins minted during the first century provide a graphic depiction of this: on the front ("obverse"), a portrait of the emperor with his titles

complex closer to the harbor and adjacent to the Church of St. Mary—which was built entirely within one of the four porticoes built around the perimeter of the courtyard surrounding the Temple of Hadrian.

FIGURE 3.17. Temple of Trajan (emperor 98–117 CE) and Zeus, Pergamum. After its construction, this temple dominated the acropolis, including the Altar of Zeus, bearing witness to the ongoing importance of the imperial cult in the early second century. (Photo by author.) See page 169 for color version.

FIGURE 3.18. An inscription from the area of the Temple of Trajan naming Trajan "lord of earth and sea" and identifying the city of Pergamum as "twice *neōkoros*." (Photo by author.)

FIGURE 3.19. Detail of the lines from the inscription (fig. 3.18) speaking of "the council and citizenry . . . of the twice *neōkoros* Pergamenes." (Photo by author.)

FIGURE 3.20. An inscription made by "the council and citizenry of the first and great metropolis of Asia and twice *neōkoros* city of the Ephesians" to honor one of its citizens. The well-preserved inscription shows the original painting of the lettering. (Photo by author.) See page 169 for color version.

FIGURE 3.21. An inscription from the Asklepion outside of Pergamum bears witness to the city's continued claim to preeminence in the province based on its devotion to the imperial cult after Ephesus was awarded its second Neokorate. Pergamum remained "first to be named 'twice temple warden.'" (Photo by author.) See page 170 for color version.

FIGURE 3.22. Denarius of Tiberius, with Peace (thought also to represent Livia, Tiberius's mother) seated on the reverse. The legend on the obverse is shorthand for "Tiberius Caesar Augustus, Son of the Deified Augustus," and the legend on the reverse for "Highest Priest." (Courtesy of Classical Numismatic Group, LLC; www.CNGcoins.com.)

(including *divi filius*, "son of the deified one," and *Pontifex Maximus*); on the reverse, a portrait of some deity, showing that his rule was grounded in the rule of the gods (or of "Fortune," or destiny). He ruled by divine right, and his achievements were signs of divine favor.

The emperor was frequently worshiped in tandem with *Dea Roma*, the personified and deified representation of Rome. The worship of Roma as a goddess was the ultimate legitimation of Roman power. Augustus refused to allow any temple to be consecrated to himself unless Roma was also included. The imperial cult thus reinforced the belief that Rome was chosen by the gods to rule the world, to subdue all nations and lead them into a golden age of lasting peace and well-being, united under her banner.

We need to remember that the imperial cult, like the cults of the traditional gods, was not merely a matter of stone temples, lifeless statues, and voiceless inscriptions passively waiting to be noticed. Priests and celebrants regularly brought these sites and their ideology to life, following a calendar of imperial celebrations, including the monthly commemoration of the reigning emperor's birthday. One contemporary Revelation scholar describes the scenes thus:

> Imperial temples and sanctuaries were wreathed with flowers. Animals were sacrificed at various altars throughout the main locations of the city, for example, the council house, temples of other deities, theatres, the main squares, stadiums, and gymnasiums. These political, religious, and public buildings were linked together by processions and dignitaries, garlanded animals being led to slaughter, and bearers of icons and symbols of the emperor. As the procession

> passed by, householders would sacrifice on small altars outside their homes. The whole city thus had opportunity to join in the celebration.[10]

The air would be filled with the sound of hymns chanted to the emperor and to the gods on behalf of the emperor, as by a community choir formed in Pergamum specifically to sing hymns to Augustus as to a god in the imperial temple. Scenes of worship centered upon the image of the emperor were both elaborate and commonplace in the experience of John and his audience.

Every glimpse of such an edifice or image, every civic festival celebrating the birthday of an emperor or a member of his household, every time a person stopped to count his change—these experiences extended invitations to the residents of these cities to remember at least a part of this official story about Roman rule: The gods in their generosity gave us Rome and her emperors to provide the gifts of stability, prosperity, safety from harm, and relief in need; thanks be to the gods! In the eyes of the local citizens and elites, participation in the cults of the emperor and Roma demonstrated appropriate gratitude to the emperor and the Roman order for maintaining the peaceful conditions that facilitated stability, even prosperity. It evidenced the piety and sense of duty that assured one's neighbors of one's commitment to do one's part to support that order on which the well-being of the local community depended. By promoting withdrawal and distance from the cult, Christians fell under their neighbors' suspicion. Christian groups could look like associations of unreliable members of the community at best, pockets of dissent and potential sedition at worst.

John's References to the Public Story

When John speaks of a "great city" sitting upon "seven hills" and having "authority over the kings of the earth" (Rev. 17:9, 17), he speaks of a reality that resonates immediately with the hearers' experience. The seven hills of Rome were, of course, celebrated in literature and coinage.[11] A yearly festival

10. Leonard L. Thompson, *The Book of Revelation: Apocalypse and Empire* (Oxford University Press, 1990), 162.

11. Literary references include Virgil, *Georgics* 2.535; *Aen.* 6.784; Ovid, *Tristia* 1.4.69; Martial, *Epigrams* 4.64.11. Plutarch (*Quaestiones romanae* 69) and Varro (*De lingua Latina* 6.24) both refer to a festival called *Septimontium*, commemorating Rome's expansion to cover its seventh hill.

in the capital commemorated Rome's expansion to enclose the seven hills within the city limits. On this basis, both Christian hearers and outsiders would immediately connect Babylon with Rome. When John speaks of a city into which the wealth of the world flowed, one would not have to be a Christian to make the obvious connection. And what an extreme makeover *Roma Aeterna* receives at John's hands!

Similarly, when John uses images from Daniel representing world empires to speak of a "beast" (compare Rev. 13:1–2 with Dan. 7:3–7), fatally wounded but healed (Rev. 13:3), worshiped by "the inhabitants of the earth" in a manner involving a cult image (13:8; see also 13:3–4, 14), and exercising authority over a multiethnic, multilingual, multinational empire (13:7), the Roman emperors were immediately available to John's hearers as plausible referents, whose cult was practiced in every one of their cities and whose rule and divinity were everywhere proclaimed.

John selected these landmarks from the landscape of first-century Roman Asia for special examination through his apocalyptic lens. Roman imperialism, with its seductive economy and blasphemous imperial cult, is a primary challenge to Christian faith and witness, as John identifies these challenges in Revelation 4–22. John raises his voice alongside those of other protestors like the authors of 4 Ezra and 2 Baruch, two contemporary Jewish apocalypses equally sharp in their criticism of Rome. John was not a solitary, raving lunatic. There were numerous others who similarly refused to allow the official picture that we have been exploring to go unchallenged. The multiplicity of voices speaking out against Rome's injustices at the close of

FIGURE 3.23. Sesterce of Vespasian, with the goddess Roma seated and reclining on Rome's seven hills. She holds a scepter as a symbol of her authority. A representation of the river Tiber as a god reclines at her feet. (Courtesy of Numismatica Ars Classica AG; auction 54, lot 361.) See page 171 for color version.

the first century, of which John's voice was one, helps us see that Jews and Christians in Asia Minor were not only concerned about local affairs, false teachers, or throwing stones at the church or synagogue across the street. The whole Roman imperial system, together with all its local manifestations, was also a major problem. And, in keeping with the claims made previously about the relevance of Revelation for its first audiences, the Christians in Roman Asia Minor did not have to look beyond their own cities to see what John was talking about, and to understand Revelation as a radical unmasking of the world around them, with all of its challenges and its temptations.

Reflection

Read through the book of Revelation with these realities in your mind. Put yourself in the place of a Christian in Ephesus or Pergamum, to the extent possible. Surround yourself in your mind with the temples to the traditional gods and to the various emperors, with the neighbors who are happy to include the acknowledgment of these gods at their private and public meals, in their business meetings, and in civic festivals. Surround yourself with the bustling activity of tradesmen and merchants and merchant marines loading their cargoes and growing wealthy from trade. Remember Antipas, whose life was forfeited because of his witness against these things.

1. How does John make you look at your world differently?
2. What questions and issues does John raise in regard to what is going on all around you?
3. What does it mean for eternity to get in bed with Rome and its imperialism now?

4

The True Center and the Unholy Scam: John's Biblical Critique of the Public Story

In the previous chapter, we looked in depth at the "public" story that sought to render Rome's worldwide domination legitimate—presenting it as an expression of the gods' providential care and a pillar for the stability and security of all peoples, tribes, nations, and languages. In this chapter, we will look at the alternative story—the very different story—that John tells, and the ways in which he works the major players of the story of Rome—the emperors, the local supporters of Roman power, and the figure of Roma herself—into that larger story.

The larger story, of course, is the story of the one God, the Creator of heaven and earth, and his past and future interventions in human history. John's story is the story of the Scriptures. He has grounded himself so fully and fervently in the traditional revelations about God, God's character, and God's vision for human community that he speaks from beginning to end in the idiom and images of the Scriptures. He cannot help but see the world through the lens of that tradition, and his Revelation extends an invitation to the churches in Asia Minor to see their local setting and their world through the lens of the scriptural revelation of God—to see their landscape anew in the light of God and of the Lamb.

What, then, does Roman Asia and the larger Roman world look like under the light of the sacred tradition and the light of the character of the God who created all that is and who is coming in judgment upon all that is?

Finding the True Center

To answer this, we need to start where John does, which is not with things earthly but with things heavenly. For the focal point of the cosmos—the center from which all things are to be measured—is not in Ephesus or Pergamum or Sardis, where our congregations live and move and go about their daily business. Nor is the center of the cosmos in Rome, where the great power brokers and shapers of the political scene wield their influence. It is not even in Jerusalem, the city at the center of John's ethnic and religious tradition. Rather, it is in the realm beyond the visible, material world.

John's visions begin at this center—at the very throne of God (Rev. 4:2). The way John unfolds his vision of the cosmos is rhetorically significant. Many modern readers jump to the dragon and beasts as the focal point of interest, but for John the key figures in this drama are not the "bad guys." God and the Lamb, not the beast, occupy center stage. This is in itself an attack on Roman imperial ideology, which depicted the emperor (and the gods that give him his power) at the center of the conceptual universe.

FIGURE 4.1. Gustave Doré's visualization of the throne of God, surrounded by countless circling throngs of angels. Illustration for Dante's *Paradiso*, Canto 31. (http://commons.wikimedia.org/wiki/File:Paradiso_Canto_31.jpg.)

FIGURE 4.2. A statue of Apollo from the Vatican Museums. Apollo wears a wreath, carries a *kithara* (a "harp"), and holds a libation bowl—three accoutrements also found in the possession of the twenty-four elders (Rev. 4:4; 5:8). (Photo by author.) See page 172 for color version.

John opens his unveiling, his apocalypse, with a vision of perfect order, with all created beings in concentric circles and spheres looking in toward the true center of the cosmos, worshiping God and the Lamb as they deserve. First a figurative door in the dome of the sky has to crack open before mortals like John and his readers can peer into that realm beyond visible realities (Rev. 4:2). There God sits enthroned, surrounded first by four "living creatures" resembling the seraphim or other angelic attendants in earlier throne visions (4:6–8; cf. Isa. 6:2–3; Ezek. 1:5–11). Seven spirits, best understood as the seven high-ranking archangels or angels of the Presence, stand next in attendance around the throne (Rev. 4:5b).[1] Twenty-four enthroned elders (4:4) form a further circle around God's throne, again quite likely representing another order of angelic beings (such as one encounters in Col. 1:16; Testament of Levi 3:8). Around these, in ever-widening circles, move angels in the ten thousands of ten thousands (5:11). All of these superhuman creatures are focused on the Enthroned One and the Lamb, offering continual worship and adoration. Finally, at the furthest reaches of this map, John places "every creature in heaven and on earth and under the earth

1. Though it has been common in the history of interpretation to identify these "seven spirits" with the Holy Spirit (through a detour to the alleged "sevenfold spirit" of the Lord in Isa. 11:2–3), the tradition of seven chief angels of the Presence was well established in John's orbit (Tob. 12:15; 1 Enoch 90:21; Targum Pseudo-Jonathan Gen. 11:7). Angels can be referred to as "spirits" or "flames of fire" as well, as in Heb. 1:7, 14 (NIV), interpreting Ps. 104:4; Jubilees 1:25; 2:2; 15:31–32; 1 Enoch 62:12; 2 Baruch 21:6. John also seems to refer to this group again as "the seven angels who stand before God" at Rev. 8:2, figures that are nowhere in this scene of beings "who stand before God" if they are not identical to the seven spirits.

and in the sea" (5:13), united in directing praise and adoration toward the center of the cosmos, God and the Lamb: "Blessing and honor and glory and power forever and ever to the One seated upon the throne and to the Lamb!" (5:13 AT). If there is a true "universal consensus," it upholds not the reign of the emperors, but the reign of the one true God (historically known as the God of Israel) and this God's Messiah.

The hymns they sing remind John's audience of the grounds for such worship and thanksgiving.

> You are worthy, our Lord and God, to receive glory and honor and power, for you created all things, and by your will they existed and were created. (4:11)

The first hymn declares that God deserves public acknowledgment (glory), honor, and power because God has created all that is. The unstated premise here is the conviction—universally held throughout the Greco-Roman world—that benefactors merit a grateful response, typically including honor and service.[2] And among benefactors, God would rank as the supreme example. The one Creator God is worthy of worship, and the benefaction of the gift of life itself requires a response of obedience, living that life in accordance with God's commandments, which include the prohibition of worshiping any other would-be divinity. It would certainly preclude using the gift of life to provoke the Giver of it!

The second hymn celebrates the unique authority that belongs by right to the Lamb:

> You are worthy to take the scroll and to break its seals, for you were slaughtered and by your blood you ransomed for God saints from every tribe and language and people and nation; you have made them to be a kingdom and priests serving our God, and they will reign on earth. . . . Worthy is the Lamb that was slaughtered to receive power and wealth and wisdom and might and honor and glory and blessing! (5:9–12)

The authority to take this scroll from the hand of God and to open its seals, we soon find out, translates to the authority to set in motion the events that bring about the final judgment upon the earthly kingdoms and that

2. For an in-depth introduction to the ethos of reciprocity in the Greco-Roman world and its implications for reading the New Testament, see David A. deSilva, *Honor, Patronage, Kinship, and Purity: Unlocking New Testament Culture*, rev. ed. (IVP Academic, 2022), 96–175.

usher in God's kingdom—to bring "the kingdom of the world" under the complete authority of "the kingdom of our Lord and of his Messiah" (11:15). This authority belongs to the Lamb "by right," because the Lamb redeemed a people for God to constitute that kingdom, giving up his own life on their behalf, fulfilling at last the promise of the creation of a priestly kingdom (as expressed in Exod. 19:6). In so doing, the Lamb exemplifies supreme beneficence, giving himself fully in the interest of the many rather than acting out of self-interest, rendering an important service to people in significant need (since "redeeming" or "ransoming" suggests a situation of significant distress). Therefore, the Lamb also merits gratitude in the highest degree.

Notice also how John has set the stage for the Lamb's coming forward. An angel issues a challenge:

> "Who is worthy to open the scroll and break its seals?" And no one in heaven or on earth or under the earth was able to open the scroll or to look into it. And I began to weep bitterly, because no one was found worthy to open the scroll or to look into it. (5:2–4)

No one can step into that silence, and for all his pretensions, the emperor, the alleged "savior" of the known world, is also unworthy of this ultimate honor. It is Jesus—the slaughtered Lamb (notably, slaughtered under Rome)—who has the greater worthiness, who has shown more worthily what it means to serve God's design for humanity and to act as a perfect benefactor. In response to the Lamb's victorious accomplishment of ransoming this people for God, John writes,

> I heard every creature in heaven and on earth and under the earth and in the sea and all that is in them, singing: "To the One seated on the throne and to the Lamb be blessing and honor and glory and might forever and ever!" (5:13)

In this picture of the cosmic order, where is there room to worship another?

It quickly becomes clear, however, that this vision of the perfectly ordered cosmos is a vision of the way things ought to be, but not of the way things are in every corner of the cosmos. The Lamb has redeemed a people out "from every tribe and language and people and nation," but this leaves other people in those tribes, language groups, peoples, and nations who are not part of that redeemed body, people who are out of line with the cosmic order in which "all creatures" acknowledge God and the Lamb with due honor and grateful obedience.

When, with John, we look away from the center back toward the earth again, we see more clearly who these deviant people are. There are some who are bucking against the "universal consensus" that acknowledges the reign of God and the Lamb. There are signs of significant pockets of resistance to, even rebellion against, the divine order. There are people who, in the face of the proclamation about this one God and even in the face of experiencing this God's judgments at the sounding of the first six of the seven trumpets (8:1–9:19),

> did not repent of the works of their hands so as to give up worshiping demons and idols of gold and silver and bronze and stone and wood, which cannot see or hear or walk, and did not repent of their murders or their sorceries or their fornication or their thefts. (9:20–21 AT)

John pulls off quite a conceptual coup. The vast majority of people living around the Mediterranean basin worshiped multiple gods and goddesses, almost always incorporating idols as visible representations of their deities into their worship sites and rituals. This was evident even in our brief surveys of the landmarks and activity in Ephesus and Pergamum. The cults of Rome and the emperors, in particular, evoked a mental picture for the worshipers in which Rome and its enthroned emperors, as the center of power in the Mediterranean, were the center of the universe. The Jews and Christians living in these cities were deviant minorities, turning away from such cultic centers to perform their own rites to their tribal God in the conceptual margins of the city.

In John's vision, however, it is the worshipers of idols that constitute the deviant minority. The hosts of heaven, together with "every creature in heaven and on earth and under the earth," recognize the true center of the cosmos, and thus where to direct adoration properly, and the minority Christian groups are attuned to this order. Those who worship the Greco-Roman divinities are the ones looking in the wrong directions and orienting themselves around false centers. They have ordered their lives around "demons," the associates of Satan, the archenemy of God and of the cosmic order (see Rev. 13:4), and they (not the Christians!) are the source of the vicious acts that erode human community, allied as they are with Satan and his party. Jewish and early Christian writers made sense of gentile religion in a number of ways. While one of these was to focus on the images that the gentiles made of their gods and the lifelessness of these images, another was to focus on the spiritual forces that lurked behind these "gods" and their images. By the first century, it was well-established in the minds of devotees of the God of Israel—the only *living* God ("the one . . . who lives forever and ever," Rev. 4:9, 10)—that the worship offered to idols was, in fact, given to demons (see Ps. 106:37; Bar. 4:6–7; 1 Cor. 10:14–21).

The dramatic action of Revelation focuses on how the forces from the heavenly "center" break into and overrun the realities around the Christian congregations in the seven cities (and, indeed, the Roman world). John narrates a future in which everything that is "out of order" is either set back in order vis-à-vis the centrality of God and the Lamb and their just requirements, or else eliminated (by virtue of being deposited in the receptacle of the lake of fire) if it resists being brought back in line. The wheels are set in motion by the opening of the seven seals that fasten the scroll shut. John does not explicitly say when this action happened, but since the Lamb's appearance in God's realm after completing his "conquest" would naturally be linked with his ascension, John's hearers might naturally think of the opening of these seals as having already been accomplished in the intervening decades. And, indeed, they would have recognized in the gallop of the four horsemen—conquest, violent bloodshed, famine, and death—forces that already had been unleashed and were active throughout living memory (6:1–8). By the time John wrote to his congregations, the space beneath the heavenly altar would have been well populated by the martyred witnesses of the Lamb, including many of the early leaders of the movement as well as the victims of Nero's brutal persecution in Rome in the mid-60s, whose memory still freshly cried for vindication (6:9–11). The only thing that John's audiences learn for certain about their own future from the opening of the first five seals is that Christ-followers would face more executions for their witness before God's final interventions to bring justice to his faithful ones: "They were told that they should rest for yet a little longer, until their fellow slaves and their brothers and sisters, who were about to be killed as they themselves had been, should be fulfilled" (6:11 AT).

The first climax in this series of seven introduces a pair of contrasting scenes in which human beings encounter God and the Lamb. The first scene—the most fully developed scene following the breaking of a seal—is one of abject terror:

> I looked on as he opened the sixth seal, and there was a great earthquake. The sun became black as funeral clothing, and the entire moon turned red as blood. The stars of the sky fell to the earth as a fig tree drops its fruit when shaken by a strong wind. The sky disappeared like a scroll being rolled up, and every

> mountain and island was moved from its place. Then the kings of the earth, the officials and the generals, the rich and the powerful, and everyone, slave and free, hid themselves in caves and in the rocks of the mountains. They called to the mountains and the rocks, "Fall on us and hide us from the face of the one seated on the throne and from the Lamb's wrath! The great day of their wrath has come, and who is able to stand?" (6:12–17 CEB)

John's audiences are themselves implicitly included in this response, for it is not only the kings and potentates, but also every "slave and free" person who trembles before God and the Lamb (6:15). This sounds like a strange counterpoint to Revelation 5:13, where "every creature" shouts in worship rather than in fear. John's presentation of universal, contradictory visions highlights the alternatives he sets before his congregations. The hearers are driven to "see" themselves in both scenes, to experience the accompanying feelings, and thus to resolve themselves to remain consistently centered on God and the Lamb in all their doings.

The scene of panic ends with the rhetorical question borrowed from an older prophetic text: "Who can stand when he appears?" (Mal. 3:2). An answer, however, emerges in the following scene of the 144,000 who receive "the seal of the living God" (Rev. 7:2) and enjoy protection from God's judgments, and even more fully in the experience of the "great crowd that no one could number" who are seen *standing* (7:9 CEB) before God's throne:

> They were from every nation, tribe, people, and language. They were standing before the throne and before the Lamb. They wore white robes and held palm branches in their hands. . . . These people have come out of great hardship. They have washed their robes and made them white in the Lamb's blood. This is the reason they are before God's throne. They worship him day and night in his temple, and the one seated on the throne will shelter them. They won't hunger or thirst anymore. No sun or scorching heat will beat down on them, because the Lamb who is in the midst of the throne will shepherd them. He will lead them to the springs of life-giving water, and God will wipe away every tear from their eyes. (7:9, 14–17 CEB)

Before the terror of the coming of God and the Lamb on the day of their wrath, a terror that is so severe that it simply cannot be faced (6:16–17), there is only one remedy, one path to relief and safety: to remain a faithful witness to God and to the Lamb, and to keep oneself from becoming entangled in the sins of the Roman imperial system, no matter what temporary disadvantages or deprivations result.

John's opening visions invite rather direct appropriation among churches in every age, since the scenes into which the readers and hearers project themselves belong, in John's own worldview and the worldview fostered by Nicene Christianity, to the eternal, cosmic realm or to the realm of the eschatological future. The vision of cosmic worship is an eternal reality, though the opening of the scroll itself marks the incursion of those heavenly realities into the sphere of history. The visions of those standing victorious before the throne of God or cowering in fear before God's burning anger on the "day of wrath" belong to the post-historical future. As such, these scenes beckon us still to imagine ourselves within them and to examine ourselves and our discipleship from their perspective.

The vision of all creation centered in worship and obediently waiting upon God and God's Messiah invites us first of all into the experience of God's throne as the pivotal center of our lives, prompting us to make this the focal point of our corporate worship and our personal prayer and meditation. John calls us to center ourselves, and to remain centered, here. This centering for John does not belong to the fleeting moments of structured times of worship, however. It is the business of God's creatures "day and night without ceasing" (4:8), which for human beings must mean bringing every facet of life into orbit around the enthroned God, centered on God, on God's prompting, on God's service. In John's vision of the cosmos, there is no room for gathering around God's throne at one time as one's cosmic center and at another time in the fellowship of idols and their worshipers.

There are prophets and teachers among the seven churches who are, in fact, promoting the opposite, domesticating the demands of a unique, Creator God to the practical needs of functioning in, and profiting from, the domination systems of the present world order and the cultic rituals that legitimate them (eating "food sacrificed to idols," Rev. 2:14, 20). John challenges us to examine whether we stand appropriately focused on God on Sunday mornings but spend most of our time (and, truth be told, some of Sunday morning as well) turning away to move into orbit around other, more local centers—our national centers, our commercial centers, our own selves—serving agendas other than God's. As I myself consider how we tend to invoke God and involve God in the religious settings of which I am a part, I find John's vision of a God-centered cosmos raising even more disturbing questions about whether or not we are guilty of treating God as if he orbited around us, expecting God to show up to do our bidding, warming our hearts here, healing us there, taking care of this concern or problem over here. John would have disciples in every age understand—and live like they understand—that they exist to do God's bidding, because God created all things for the doing of *God's* will and for God's good pleasure (4:11).

Roman Imperialism: The Untold Story

When John takes us to look even closer into the activity of the world in rebellion against God, we see a movement afoot to steal away the worship due the one God and to draw as many people as possible into a lie that leads them away from the true center. John thoroughly dismantles the dominant culture's story. From the point of view of the throne of the one God and his Christ, Roman power, the emperor, and the worship offered to both everywhere look quite different from the way the Christians' neighbors view these things. Indeed, by reminding his churches of the awe and gratitude due the Creator God and the Redeemer Lamb, the genuine Savior and Son of God (Rev. 4–5), John laid the groundwork for evoking indignation against the pretensions of promoters of the cult of Rome and the *Augusti* (the collective body of emperors) in these later visions.

First, in Revelation 12–13, John completely rewrites the ideology of the heads of empire. John takes the four beasts of Daniel 7, representing in sequence the kingdoms of Babylon, Persia, Greece, and Alexander's successors, and combines them into a single, monstrous hybrid to represent Roman rule and Rome's heads of state. Roman imperialism brings together all that the previous empires had contained in terms of geography, power, and bestial corruption. The unnatural, animal imagery hides the humanness of the emperor and negates any legitimate claims he might have to the gratitude or loyalty of the audiences. The *Augusti* appear as a monstrous aberration, prodigious in the worst sense. Like Daniel before him in regard to earlier empires, John invites his audience to regard the character and rule of Rome's emperors as something out of harmony with the divine and natural orders.

The "beast's" origins are not what the public story claims. The rule of the *Augusti* does not spring from some benign Providence seeking to order human life well, but from the rebellion of Satan, the source of all chaos and disorder, against God. John crafts a new backstory for their emergence in Revelation 12:1–18. Satan, presented here as a seven-headed dragon, sets himself in opposition to God's anointed one but is thwarted in his attempts to destroy him (12:1–6). This is a highly condensed and figurative "prequel" to the Lamb's triumphant entrance into heaven (5:1–6). In a second scene, the dragon and the angels that have aligned themselves with his rebellion are defeated by the loyal angelic forces of Michael and cast down from heaven to the earth (12:7–12). After this degrading defeat, Satan invests his power in this "beast"—his clone and vice-regent on earth—as part of his last-ditch attempt to deceive people and lead them astray from God's truth, knowing "that his time is short" (12:12): "The dragon stood on the seashore, and I saw a beast coming up out of the sea. . . . The dragon gave it his power, throne, and great authority" (12:18–13:2 CEB). The Christians' neighbors would affirm that Zeus gave the emperors their authority. John reframes this by drawing upon the conviction that the worship given to idols is given to demonic forces, with Satan, the chief of demons, masquerading as Zeus, the chief of the "gods." Therefore, Satan ultimately stands behind Roman power as its source.

The emperors themselves are not pious figures or mediators of divine favor, as the public image of them declares. Rather, they are fountainheads of blasphemy against God (13:1, 5, 6). The emperor's divine titles (typically including "son of a god," in Latin, *divi filius*; in Greek, *huios theou*) are illegitimate, the "names of blasphemy" that offend the Most High. Flattering courtiers in Rome and local authorities in Asia Minor addressed their emperors as "lord and God"; what was for most of Asia Minor a matter of gratitude and welcome security was, for John, an insult to the one Lord and one God in the highest degree. Indeed, many of the titles ascribed to God and the Lamb throughout Revelation are stolen back by John from the emperor for the true God and his Anointed One. The title "Lord of lords," for example, was ascribed to the emperor; the acclamations of God and Christ as "worthy" (4:11; 5:9) echo the sorts of acclamations with which citizens greeted their emperor. And Zeus, or Jupiter, the highest god whose power stood behind the emperor, was lauded with the formula "Zeus was, Zeus is, Zeus will be, O great Zeus!" (as in Pausanias, *Descr.* 10.12.10).[3] This is taken over by John and transformed for the one God, "who is and was and is coming" (Rev. 1:4, 8 CEB). The shift (from "will be" to "is coming") is significant: This God is on the way to encounter his creation and intervene once more in human affairs.

John challenges the public narrative that Augustus received "universal consent" to rule as a response to his beneficence and investment of himself in the public good. In John's presentation, "in amazement the whole

3. M. Eugene Boring, Klaus Berger, and Carsten Colpe, eds., *Hellenistic Commentary to the New Testament* (Abingdon, 1995), 560.

earth followed the beast. . . . They worshiped the beast, saying, 'Who is like the beast, and who can fight against it?'" (13:3–4). The second part of this rationale for worship is telling: Whereas the Lamb's authority is acknowledged by universal consent on the more noble and praiseworthy basis of his others-centered sacrifice, the emperors received and maintain it on the basis of military might and the use of violence as the mechanism for unifying multiple peoples, languages, nations, and tribes into "empire" (see also 18:24).

The beast and Satan—God's enemies and the Lamb's rivals for sway over humankind—enjoy what they do not deserve—namely, worship. John uses parody to highlight the counterfeit nature of the worship going on all around the churches. The beast worshipers ask, "Who is like the beast?" (13:4), a rhetorical question implying that there is no one equal to this great and powerful being. Throughout the Scriptures, however, John's audience would have encountered this same rhetorical question but would have heard it raised in regard to the one God:

> Who is like you, O Lord, among the gods?
>   Who is like you, majestic in holiness? (Exod. 15:11)
>
> O Lord, who is like you? (Ps. 35:10)
>
> O God, who is like you? (Ps. 71:19)

The inhabitants of the earth acclaim the beast using a phrase, then, stolen from the worship of God, even as the worship offered to the beast and the dragon itself is worship stolen from the God to whom it is uniquely due as Creator of all that is, sharpening the impropriety and injustice of this cult of the beast.

In a parody of Christ's legitimate bringing together of a people for God from every "tribe and language and people and nation" (Rev. 5:9), the beast from the sea seeks to exercise rule over the members of every "tribe and people and language and nation" (13:7), and indeed the imperial cult was a powerful tool for unifying the many different people groups now brought under the aegis of Rome. A second, local beast organizes religious cult for the first beast, making the worship of the beast a requirement for continued economic and physical well-being:

> I saw another beast coming up from the earth. . . . It also makes the earth and those who live in it worship the first beast, whose fatal wound was healed. . . . It told those who live on earth to make an image for the beast who had been wounded by the sword and yet came to life again. . . . It forces everyone—the small and great, the rich and poor, the free and slaves—to have a mark put on

> their right hand or on their forehead. It will not allow anyone to make a purchase or sell anything unless the person has the mark with the beast's name or the number of its name. (13:11–17 CEB)

Again, this is a reversal of the majority view of the imperial cult, understood as a pious response of gratitude to a great benefactor—something freely, even enthusiastically and rightly, offered to the one seated upon the throne in Rome. John presents it rather as an imposition from those in power, not a voluntary cult, giving poignant expression to the pressures to participate that Christians felt and would soon feel all the more.

Once again, the ultimate recipient of such cult is not a benign deity but the dragon, the enemy of God, whose worship is linked to that of the beast (13:4), even as the cults of the traditional gods were frequently linked to the imperial cult: "All the earth marveled after the beast and they worshiped the dragon, because he gave authority to the beast, and they worshiped the beast" (13:3–4 AT). In John's understanding, it is not the Christians who act seditiously by withdrawing from participation in the cults of Rome and the Roman gods but the supporters of Rome who rebel against the rule of the Most High God and his Anointed. The only kind of person who could participate in such cults is a person whose name "hadn't been written—from the time the earth was made—in the scroll of life of the Lamb who was slain" (13:8 CEB).

John uses Nero as a kind of symbol to characterize the institution of the emperor as a whole. While the "mortal wound" affects the beast as a whole and not merely one of its heads (13:12, 14), the sword blow to one of its heads (13:3) cannot help but recall Nero's suicide. The detail that a future "head" will come, in fact, from one of those that have fallen, is perhaps the clearest echo of the popular legend of "Nero returning" or even "Nero revived" in the book (17:11). Three individuals are known to have actually pretended to be Nero in the decades following his death, gaining support for their ultimately futile attempts to take the imperial throne away from the Flavian emperors.[4] Around the turn of the second century, Dio Chrysostom attests to the fact that the belief that Nero was alive "out there somewhere" persisted to his day (*Oration* 21.10).

But Nero is not merely one aberrant head among others: He gives the beast its character. When John comes to the topic of the beast's number, he

4. Their stories can be found in Tacitus, *Hist.* 1.2.1; 2.8–9; Suetonius, *Nero* 57.2; and Dio Cassius, *Hist.* 63.9.3; 66.19.3.

says, "This calls for wisdom. Let the one who understands calculate the beast's number, for it's a human being's number. Its number is six hundred sixty-six" (13:18 CEB). John is inviting his audiences to participate in a common kind of game in the Greco-Roman world known as *gematria*. Latin, Greek, and Hebrew all use letters to represent not only sounds but also numerals. Thus every word or name could also be thought of as having a numerical sum. A graffito scratched into some plaster in Pompeii reads, "I love her whose number is 545." Several similar graffiti have been found in the excavated areas of the forum in Smyrna: "I love her whose number is 1308"; "I love her whose number is 731." The amorous vandal thus bears witness to his crush, but the passersby, if sufficiently interested, would have to work to figure out who in Pompeii or Smyrna was the object of this crush. They could start adding up the numerical values of the letters in the names of the women they knew to see if they could land on one that matched the sum. In the case of "her whose number is 1308," one candidate might be the pretty girl who works in the tavern who was named *Tyche* after the goddess of destiny. The letters in her name add up to the required sum (*tau* = 300, *upsilon* = 400, *chi* = 600, *ēta* = 8). Some examples take on a political edge. Suetonius records a popular slur that circulated after Agrippina the Elder's death: "A calculation new—Nero his mother slew" (*Nero* 39.2). In the original Greek phrase, the letters in each of the two parts of the saying add up to the same total—namely, 1005.

When John identifies the "number" of the beast's name as 666 (Rev. 13:18; 15:2), he is inviting his audience to play this game. In their reflections on this puzzle, early church fathers offered a number of possible solutions based on Latin and Greek. The most durable solution that has emerged, however, is based on the Hebrew transliteration for "Nero Caesar." Based on the Greek spelling (*Nerōn Kaisar*), this comes out as *nrwn qsr* and the letters add up just right:

nun	50
resh	200
waw	6
nun	50
qoph	100
samekh	60
resh	200
Total	**666**

What makes this solution particularly attractive is the fact that it also accounts for a variant in the Greek manuscript tradition that gives the number of the beast as 616. If the Hebrew followed the Latin spelling of Nero's name (*Nero* rather than *Nerōn*, as in the Greek), the second *nun* is omitted, and the sum stands at 616. John thus invites the hearers to see in Nero—and in Nero's distinctive persecution of Roman Christians and their leaders—the true character of imperial rule, bare, exposed in all its ugliness and its opposition to the reign of Christ.

In this subversive portrait, John also questions the public claims made about the *Pax Augusta* or *Pax Romana*—a "peace" secured and preserved by Augustus and his successors, a benefit of unity under Roman rule. A prominent element of Roman imperial ideology was the claim that the rise of the principate had brought "peace" to the *orbis terrarum*. John exposes *Pax Romana* and *Pax Augusta* to be bald-faced lies. He does not allow his hearers to ignore the fact that a great deal of violence has gone into creating and sustaining the empire, for example, in the brutal suppression of the Jewish Revolt. How is it truly a matter of "peace" if you use overwhelming force to subdue a country that never wished to be a part of your empire in the first place?

The *Pax Romana* is also, in fact, a time of "wag[ing] war on the saints" (Rev. 13:7), "mak[ing] war" with the witnesses of Jesus, conquering, and killing them (11:7). With the opening of the fifth seal, John identifies a pressing cause for the judgments that are coming:

> I saw under the altar those who had been slaughtered on account of the word of God and the witness they had given. They cried out with a loud voice, "Holy and true Master, how long will you wait before you pass judgment? How long before you require justice for our blood, which was shed by those who live on earth?" Each of them was given a white robe, and they were told to rest a little longer, until their fellow servants and brothers and sisters—who were about to be killed as they were—were finished. (6:9–11 CEB)

The souls of Christian martyrs cry out for justice; later, two angels will praise the justice of God for punishing "Babylon" and its allies for violently snuffing out the lives of saints and prophets (16:5–7; 18:24). While it is unlikely that Revelation was written during a period of open persecution, the memory of the Christian holocaust in Rome, as well as more local and individual actions against Christians such as Antipas (2:13), had not dissipated in John's mind. Roman rule is the rule of violence, spilling not only the blood of holy ones and the witnesses of Jesus (17:6) but of "all who have been slain upon the earth" (18:23–24). It is a time in which those destined for slaughter by the sword and for captivity meet their destiny (13:10). Moreover, the guardians of the "Roman peace" are the pawns of Satan, deployed as part of a last-ditch effort within a cosmic revolt that continues to play itself out as Revelation nears its climax. This portrait of a world, indeed a cosmos, at war evokes an attitude of resistance against the forces that John places in the enemy's camp, steering the audience away from cooperation and compromise.

And what of *Roma Aeterna*, "Eternal Rome," the beneficent goddess whose worship was everywhere yoked to the cult of the emperor? John creates one of the most memorable—and negative—pictures of Rome in extant literature. He tells a very different story about the mission and the destiny of *Roma Aeterna* from the one heard in Virgil's *Aeneid* or Plutarch's *On the Fortune of Rome*.

First, John presents the goddess Roma in very different dress. No longer wearing the modest toga of the goddess worshiped in the Temple of Rome and Augustus in Pergamum, nor even the austere military garb in which she appears on the reverse of the famous *Dea Roma* coin (see fig. 3.23 above), here she's dressed in her evening wear, sporting the lingerie of a self-employed courtesan and plying her trade with the utmost success.

FIGURE 4.3. *The Whore of Babylon* (1809) by William Blake. See page 170 for color version.

Her impact on the civilized world is entirely negative. Her résumé includes plundering the wealth of the provinces to satisfy her taste for luxury; murdering countless holy ones, witnesses to Jesus, and others who have dissented against or hindered her practices; and seducing the leaders of the inhabited world into forming unholy alliances to promote their collective self-indulgent practices. There is nothing here of Roma as the chosen vessel by means of which Providence renews a golden age; rather, her cup is full of abominations and the unclean residue of Rome's fornication.

John helps his audiences to look at Rome and Roman imperialism especially through the lens of the Hebrew prophets, who had long ago spoken against the self-serving practices of empires as contrary to God's goodwill for human beings in every nation. A great deal of material in Revelation 17–18 is drawn from the oracles spoken against historic Babylon (Jer. 25; 50–51; Isa. 13; 21; 47) and Tyre (Isa. 23; Ezek. 26–28)—ancient cities at the hearts of Iron Age empires. In particular, John accuses Rome of (1) violence against dissenters, especially against Jews and Christians; (2) economic exploitation, nurturing a system that caters to the luxury of the powerful at the expense of the many; and (3) idolatrous presumption in its claims on its own behalf. John develops each of these in such a way as to arouse indignation against Roman imperialism, supporting his call to Christians to keep themselves free from supporting or participating in such an unjust system of domination.

John gives attention throughout Revelation to Rome's violence, refusing to allow the public rhetoric of "peace" or "stability" to mask the violence with which that "peace" has been forged and continues to be maintained. The "mother of whores" is "drunk with the blood of the saints and the blood of the witnesses to Jesus" (Rev. 17:5, 6). She is responsible for "the blood of prophets and of saints and of all who have been slaughtered on earth" (18:24), and this very fact necessitates divine vengeance upon Rome, just as it did upon historic Babylon (18:20; see also 6:9–11; 16:5–7).

Empire is forged out of conquest. A few territories came under Roman control peaceably. More, however, were "taken" by military force, as commemorative issues of imperial-period coins attest—the "taking" of Egypt and Armenia during Augustus's reign or the "taking" of Judea as a consequence of suppressing the First Jewish Revolt (*Aegypto Capta*, a minting featured under Octavian in 28 BCE; *Armenia Capta*, another minting under Augustus; *Iudaea Capta*, from multiple mintings commemorating the suppression of the First Jewish Revolt). Such conquests came with heavy casualties. John's scenes of blood filling valleys and endless flocks of carrion birds gathering to feast on the flesh of kings and soldiers are not products of apocalyptic imagination. They were available to see throughout John's lifetime (for example, in the Jewish Revolt or the suppression of smaller revolts throughout the East). Most criminals deemed seditious died by one of the most economical and cruel forms of punishment ever devised—economical because it required only some reusable wood and nails, but lasting for days as a deterrent to others who might disturb the Roman peace. The bloodbath in Rome targeting Christians under Nero showed the fragility of the protection afforded by law, long remaining a traumatic blot on the memory of Roman rule among conscientious Christians. Even a man as highly placed in the empire as the Roman historian Tacitus could see what Rome looked like "from the outside." Imagining how a German chieftain would have commented on the advancing Roman army, he writes: "To robbery, butchery, and rapine, they give the lying name of 'government'; they create a desert and call it 'peace'" (*Agr.* 30).[5]

FIGURE 4.4. Sesterce of Vespasian. The legend on the reverse reads, *Iudaea Capta*, "Judea Taken." A Jewish male captive stands beside a palm tree with his hands bound behind him; a Jewish female (perhaps representing the province itself) sits on the ground and mourns. The minting commemorates Vespasian and Titus's suppression of the Jewish Revolt of 66–70 CE. (Courtesy of Classical Numismatic Group, LLC; www.CNGcoins.com.)

John criticizes the Roman imperial economy as a system of self-interest structured chiefly to benefit Rome. The elites and inhabitants of Rome consumed disproportionate wealth and goods in great measure to indulge excessive desires and cravings (what John calls "luxury" in Rev. 18:3, 7), while the poor in Rome's provinces were often short even on the necessities of life. The gaudiness of the great prostitute, draped in luxurious clothing ("purple and scarlet"), richly adorned ("gold and jewels and pearls"), and sporting luxury goods (not just a cup, but a "golden cup"; 17:4) highlights the visceral commitment to excess and self-indulgence that John saw in the Roman economy.

He captures this economic parasitism again in his focus on the extensive cargoes flowing from the ports throughout the known world, taking both staples (like grain and oil) and luxury items away from the provinces, where they are produced, to satiate a single city's cravings:

> Cargoes of gold and silver and precious stone and pearls and linen and purple and silk and scarlet and every fragrant wood, and every ivory item and every

5. Tacitus, *The Agricola and the Germania*, trans. H. Mattingly (Penguin, 1970), 81, slightly modified.

> vessel made from costly wood and bronze and iron and marble, and cinnamon and spice and incense and myrrh and frankincense and wine and olive oil and fine flour and wheat and cattle and sheep and horses and carriages and slaves, even human lives. (18:12–13 AT)

We should bear in mind that part of what Rome enjoyed came to her by way of trade, but another large part came by way of tribute—the enormous sums of money that each province collected and sent to Rome for the support of Rome's army, Rome's empire-wide building and military operations, and Rome's lifestyle.

The Roman economy included the provision of free grain and oil for the city of Rome's two hundred thousand families on the "dole"— a perk of living in the capital of the empire. As John watches the cargoes of "wine and olive oil and fine flour and wheat" streaming toward Rome (18:13 AT), he watches the prices of staples like barley and wheat rise in the provinces where the grains are grown. Rome purchased these grains inexpensively from the provinces in fixed minimum quantities and at fixed prices. This meant that the residents of the provinces often had to pay inflated prices for the insufficient amounts of grain that were left, and in times of shortage, went without. The situation was made worse as local landowners used more and more of their land to produce crops that brought in a better financial yield per arable acre. Market demands made the production of oil and wine far more attractive, often leading to scarcity in the essentials of wheat and barley in the provinces. Revelation 6:5–6 reflects a situation in which the prices of grain staples are grossly inflated, while production of oil and wine proceeds unabated.

> When [the Lamb] opened the third seal, I heard the third living creature say, "Come!" So I looked, and there was a black horse. Its rider held a balance for weighing in his hand. I heard what sounded like a voice from among the four living creatures. It said, "A quart of wheat for a denarion, and three quarts of barley for a denarion, but don't damage the olive oil and the wine." (6:5–6 CEB)

John calls attention to the parasitic side of the Roman imperial economy, countering any feelings of gratitude toward Rome by drawing attention to the pervasive self-interest that underlay Roman rule. Roma is presented as an anti-benefactor, whose influence and interventions ultimately seek to secure self-serving ends. John includes no notice of anything Rome has done purely on behalf of her subjects. The emphasis on luxury, intemperance, and conspicuous consumption nurtures indignation, as Rome is seen to consume far more of the world's goods than any one city ought, enjoying more than is due—and often to the detriment of the provinces under her far-from-beneficent rule. If Rome brings prosperity, she does so only to the merchants and shipmasters and others who profit (or profiteer) as they direct the world's wealth and resources to her ravenous maw.

The Roman economy was, furthermore, built and maintained upon the backs of enslaved persons, humans sufficiently dehumanized to be spoken of as simply "bodies" or, in Aristotle's infamous phrase, "living tools."[6] Approximately one-quarter of the population of the empire was enslaved. While the enslaved lived under conditions that ran the gamut from desperate to luxurious, they shared this basic definition and the vulnerability it implied for their identity and security as persons. John draws attention to this facet of the Roman economy—indeed, its bedrock—by listing "bodies, that is, human lives" (18:13) in the inventory of the cargo that streams toward Rome from every quadrant of the *orbis terrarum*. In his list of twenty-eight items, John has given "bodies" the climactic position by placing it last and has heightened emphasis further by providing this brief gloss. By naming first-century enslaved persons not merely as "bodies" (*somata*)—the common designation—but also "human souls," John reminds the readers of the humanity of the people that Rome has commodified (18:13).[7]

The Roman economy also undermined resistance to Roman domination among non-Roman elites by cultivating their desire for what Rome had and could provide for her willing partners. John may have this in mind as he speaks of "Babylon" seducing the kings and the inhabitants of the earth. The Roman historian Tacitus, writing perhaps only a decade after John, attests to the fact that growing fond of and accustomed to the luxury goods and entertainments introduced with the Roman presence undermined resistance to Roman rule. As he writes his histories, he imagines a general among the north German tribes exhorting his people: "Tear yourselves from those pleasures which Romans find to be a more effective instrument of domination than

6. Aristotle, *Politics* 1.2.4; *Nicomachean Ethics* 8.11.6. For a brief introduction to slavery in the Roman Empire, see deSilva, *Honor, Patronage, Kinship, and Purity*, 215–20. For a more thorough treatment, see Christy Cobb and Katherine A. Shaner, eds., *Ancient Slavery and Its New Testament Contexts* (Eerdmans, 2025); and for a well-informed, imaginative immersion into that experience, see John Byron, *A Week in the Life of a Slave* (IVP Academic, 2019).

7. Clarice Martin, "Polishing the Unclouded Mirror: A Womanist Reading of Revelation 18:13," in *From Every People and Nation: The Book of Revelation in Intercultural Perspective*, ed. David Rhoads (Fortress, 2005), 89.

arms" (*Hist.* 4.64.3).[8] The Romans might strategically introduce luxury items and offer the "privilege" of Greek and Roman education for the children of local elites in places where there was resistance in order to achieve by such seduction what force could not achieve as efficiently.

The wealth to be enjoyed by participating in the larger global economy was, as far as John was concerned, a dangerous lure toward sharing in the violence and political injustice that undergirded such an economy, as well as sharing in the economic injustice that allowed the resources and produce of the provinces to be siphoned off to satisfy the immoderate cravings of Rome's inhabitants and worldwide elite. John understood long before the modern era that a person cannot share in the profits of domination without also sharing in responsibility for its crimes: "Come out of her, my people, so that you don't take part in her sins and don't receive any of her plagues" (Rev. 18:4 CEB).

And, of course, Rome claimed honor beyond what was rightly hers to claim (Rev. 18:7), and the cult of the goddess Roma would have been an especially egregious offense in John's eyes. Related to this charge is the presumption inherent in the public discourse about Rome as the "Eternal City," *Roma Aeterna*, claiming for Rome what has never belonged to any kingdom or empire before her: "In her heart she says, 'I sit like a queen! I'm not a widow. I'll never see grief.' This is why her plagues will come in a single day—deadly disease, grief, and hunger. She will be consumed by fire because the Lord God who judges her is powerful" (Rev. 18:7–8 CEB). Such arrogance signals Rome's refusal to apply the lessons of history to a more humble and humane rule.

John knows a God who allots to all kingdoms their times and seasons, and history has never known a kingdom that has failed to fall from its height into obscurity and subjugation to other kingdoms. God intervenes to bring low those rulers or empires that forget and affront God's sovereign oversight. Rome's claims about its divinity and destiny are textbook examples of the arrogant presumption of imperialist thinking. John exposes these pretensions in his vision of Rome's demise, which will reveal the emptiness of Rome's claims to "empire without limit" in favor of the persistent truth that all human domination systems run their course. Every seat of empire, no matter how prosperous at its peak, will one day sit as a ruin, and Rome will be no different (Rev. 18:2). The "Eternal City" stands under God's imminent judgment, sentenced already to destruction for her crimes against "saints

8. Tacitus, *The Histories*, trans. Kenneth Wellesley (Penguin, 1975), 249.

and apostles and prophets" (18:20), and will surely go up in smoke and be laid desolate rather than live up to its name (18:8, 9, 18; 19:3).

The scene of the great prostitute stripped naked, devoured by her allies, and burned up (17:16–17) is John's final answer to Rome's self-glorifying propaganda. At the level of John's metaphorical language, this is a truly disturbing scene that resonates all too well with countless instances of violence against women in real life, particularly honor killings that have nearly matched this scene for brutality. John crafts this image, however, in response to the images that populate Rome's propaganda concerning its "empire without limit." Museums throughout the Mediterranean bear witness to Rome's standard depiction of provinces in friezes or reliefs as female figures, often partially naked, often being violently subjugated by a Roman emperor. John turns that imagery back upon the perpetrator of such violence against nations and people groups around the Mediterranean that would have preferred *not* to have been subjugated to the Roman Empire.

Exerting control and maintaining peace through violent suppression of dissent, promoting an economy arranged for the great benefit of the few, and prominently using religious language and ritual to legitimate these arrangements—these are both the genius of Rome and the heap of her sins for which John excoriates her. To enter into partnership with Rome is to fall victim to its deceit (Rev. 18:23), which intoxicates the ignorant (17:2), and thus to be united with her in her sins and their punishment at the hands of the just and judging God (18:4).

John tells his audiences how the story must end. Babylon is judged at last and left a wasteland (Rev. 18:2–3, 21–24). God's Messiah returns to execute judgment upon all the forces hostile to God's rule (19:11–21). Finally, a truly new society is founded—the new Jerusalem—which exists for the healing of the nations rather than for their conquest and exploitation (21:1–22:5). All claims made on behalf of traditional Greco-Roman religion and on behalf of Roman imperialism are swept aside—or, better, exposed in the light of Scripture and in the light of the God that Scripture proclaims.

Applying John's Lenses to Our Landscape

How would we apply John's critique of Roman imperialism and call for faithful response in the midst of the same to a modern context, if we resist the approach that seeks to name some person, country, or group "the beast" and some modern entity "Babylon"? I would suggest that John would have us subject our own social, economic, and political systems, and our involvement in them (both as individual disciples and as collective Christian bodies), to the same scrutiny that John subjected those of his own time, and to do this on the same basis. That basis would be the scriptural revelation of God's priorities and agenda for human community, and God's commendation or censure of the practices that promote or impede God's priorities and agenda. Revelation, therefore, suggests a model for ongoing examination and critique of our social, political, economic, and ideological contexts in light of the scriptural revelation. It calls us also to discern the responses that would most embody a faithful witness to God's purposes and that even contribute to the creation of experiences, however fleeting, of the wholeness and justice central to God's purposes for humanity.

Thus John's precedent in Revelation summons us to ask: How do our country's economic practices, political entanglements, and ideologies look when measured up against the Israelite prophets, Jesus's teachings and example, and John's critique of his own imperial context? What values have we—as individual disciples and as groups of disciples ("churches")—internalized, and in what directions are we pulled, that run counter to the call of God to holiness and justice, to allegiance to the global family of faith, to setting the kingdom of God first? This calls for careful study both of the Scriptures, the frame of reference from which the examination takes place, and the real-life practices of our context and their effects on human beings within and outside our systems.

In this process, it is of the utmost importance that we listen to voices "from outside" our own orbits if we are ever going to get some perspective on the systems of which we are a part and on the values and ways of doing things that we never think to question. John, himself in all probability an outsider to Roman Asia Minor, was able to bring a perspective to the situation of Christians in Roman Asia Minor that they themselves were not able to arrive at on their own. In my seminary classroom, my American students and I have frequently benefited from listening to international students as they share their perspectives on the United States and on the church in the United States. They are often able to pinpoint inconsistencies between our practice and the scriptural vision that we overlook because of our socialization into our own country's values and practices. We benefit in the classroom even more regularly from conversations between persons from very different social locations within the American context where, for example, people from the inner city are able to help people in rural contexts see the realities more clearly than the images of the same portrayed in the media (or as imagined as a result of personal prejudices), or where people from near-invisible minorities like Indigenous Americans can bear witness to experiences of conquest and marginalization that call our public discourse about America into stark question.[9] Christians in church settings often have to work a lot harder to gain this perspective, since congregations are often among the most homogeneous groups in our context. Or to put this more directly in the words of Martin Luther King Jr.'s prophetic indictment: "11:00 on Sunday morning is one of the most segregated hours . . . in Christian America."[10]

And, of course, Scripture itself speaks a perennial "voice from outside," if we attend to it on its own terms. Again because of our immersion, often from birth, in the assumptions, values, goals, and practices of our own society and its systems, we tend to domesticate the voice of Scripture so that Scripture can live in the house we have built in our society. We need, rather, to invite Scripture to tell us how to rebuild the house from new foundations. One strategy for pushing past this is to be particularly attentive to the places where Jesus, Paul, James, or John rub us the wrong way. Where do we say, in response to something we're reading in the New Testament, "No, he can't possibly mean that"? Where do we jump to find some reason to blunt the force of the challenge or demand the text poses, so that we can move on without letting that word change the way we think, live, or relate to others? Where do we find ourselves making excuses for our country ("Nations have to do that kind of thing") or for ourselves ("We've got to be practical as well, and not get carried away with this religion stuff")?

In some instances, the discomfort in the encounter comes from our awareness, two thousand years later, that not even the authors of Scripture completely escaped the assumptions, values, and practices of their own social world (such as their assumptions about slavery and gender roles), and so our hearing and following of their voices must be tempered accordingly. Often, however, I would expect such instances of discomfort to draw our attention to the ways in which we have drunk deeply from Babylon's cup and are tempted to remain in our stupor. In such encounters, we need to

9. See, for example, L. Daniel Hawk, *Undoing Manifest Destiny: Settler America, Christian Colonists, and the Pursuit of Justice* (IVP Academic, 2026).

10. "Meet the Press," April 17, 1960, https://www.youtube.com/watch?v=1q881g1L_d8. The maxim, however, appears to have a prehistory.

allow the words of Jesus, Paul, John, and the rest to strike us with full force, so as to sober us up and get us ready to stand before God at his coming with confidence, rather than in terror. John's model further challenges us to look at our world *consistently* in light of the witness of Scripture and the Spirit to what God values and what God desires for human community, not shifting gears between a religious mode and a "practical" mode.

It might be of some benefit to look more closely at one particular example. Given John's interest in economic values and practices, among many other interests, I will take consumerism—and the ways in which this secular mindset and practice has infiltrated church culture—for this example. According to sociologist Barry Harvey,

> Christians in North America constitute, for the most part, a population that is not clearly distinguished from non-Christian North Americans in the modern world, assuming along with virtually everyone else that their purpose in life is to pursue their own interests in every sphere allotted to them by the institutions of our commercial republic. A majority of those who continue to call themselves Christian "retain a vague notion of religious identity but their lives are distinctively secular, with the experience of God in worship and prayer not figuring very prominently in all that they do. Increasingly these nominal Christian . . . Americans embrace the heady hedonism and narcissism of popular culture and do not see that this contradicts biblical faith." . . . Firmly ensconced in the well-worked tracks of the City, they regard religion almost exclusively as a private and inward matter, quite often as a form of therapy designed to make their lives more fulfilling. They see little or nothing wrong in regarding the church as simply another vendor of goods and services.[11]

Harvey observes that many American Christians live (and even think) in a way that agrees with the dominant culture's relegation of religion to the private, internal sphere, viewing religion as a commodity of self-help and self-actualization. Their approach to religion and to religious communities agrees with the "commodification" of religion and religious involvement as practices and experiences to be evaluated on the basis of how well they enhance one's sense of gratification and fulfillment. The testimonies that "I got a lot out of that service" and the complaint that "I don't get much out of going to that service" equally demonstrate the elevation of the "values" of

11. Barry A. Harvey, *Another City: An Ecclesiological Primer for a Post-Christian World* (Trinity Press International, 1999), 3, quoting Vigen Guroian, *Ethics After Christendom* (Eerdmans, 1994), 89.

consumerism and gratification as the uniting principles that join American Christians in solidarity with their non-Christian fellow Americans, who could evaluate their commitments and involvements in much the same way.

To the extent that this evaluation rings true, Christians are failing both to experience and to bear witness to the alternative orientation to the world (and to the problem of self) that Jesus models and promotes when he empties himself, gives his life for the life of the world, and calls followers to deny themselves and find fullness in giving themselves away. One way to speak about the problem of "self" would be to speak about the problem of emptiness, the lack of fulfillment and fullness with which people wrestle. The legacy of modernity is "a self without substance, frantically searching for something, anything, to fill it up."[12] As psychotherapist Philip Cushman writes,

> The self has become empty in part because of the loss of family, community, and tradition. It is a self that seeks the experience of being continually filled up by consuming goods, calories, experiences, politicians, romantic partners, and empathic therapists in an attempt to combat the growing alienation and fragmentation of its era.[13]

A complex system—our consumerist economy—has grown up around this problem, as we have historically continued to go to the same well-worn ruts to try to fill the emptiness. But there is something even more insidious at work here, which reveals the demonic character of "domination systems" taking on a life of their own and preying on the very people who inhabit those systems. Whole sectors of industry (particularly their propaganda divisions, whether called "marketing" or "advertising") work daily to keep us traveling in these ruts, so as to keep the consumerist economy going and growing, perpetuating the lies about how to fill that emptiness. Cushman writes, "This is a powerful illusion. And what fuels the illusion, what impels the individual into this illusion, is the desperation to fill up the empty self."[14] It is in the system's interests to perpetuate the emptiness and promote consumerism as the cure, since the "post-World War II economy . . . is dependent on the continual consumption of nonessential and quickly obsolete items and experiences."[15] Powerful subsystems thus cooperate in the production

12. Harvey, *Another City*, 8.

13. Philip Cushman, "Why the Self Is Empty: Toward a Historically Situated Psychology," *American Psychologist* 45 (1990): 599–611, esp. 600.

14. Cushman, "Why the Self Is Empty," 606.

15. Cushman, "Why the Self Is Empty," 600.

and maintenance of emptiness in the self, distracting attention and energy away from those pursuits that might lead to fullness (and to correcting the sociohistorical factors that have led to our widespread experience of emptiness) for the sake of amassing the wealth, goods, and experiences that will not fill their members' own emptiness. In this way, consumerist America becomes another example of the sociological dictum, "Each society produces the men it needs" in order for the society, the system, to continue.[16] It also becomes another example of enslavement—of the advertising mogul as much as the shopaholic—to the "powers and principalities," to supra-social forces, the human origins of which are now hidden and whose mandates go unquestioned. John himself came fairly close to this diagnosis in regard to the Christians in Laodicea, whose attempts to make themselves "full"—as their non-Christian Laodicean neighbors defined fullness—obscured their own awareness of their ongoing emptiness (Rev. 3:17), which could only be filled by participating in an entirely different economy (3:18).

Is there an alternative? Following John's method, we would look to the prophets' and Jesus's prescriptions about the acquisition and use of wealth and property, and we might even take the risk of understanding them at face value and living them out. This could not be done within the typical social and economic structures of our society, hence Jesus's maxims concerning the impossibility of putting new wine into old wineskins. It would require searching out a new ordering of community that would make it possible to live out those directions regarding wealth and property, sharing and consumption, hence the formation of new wineskins that could contain a new wine—new structures that could support a new way of living. Such a community would embrace practices that prioritized the quest for spiritual, social, and relational progress (seeking first "God's kingdom and his justice; Matt. 6:33 AT) over the quest for capital and consumer goods. It would prioritize sharing with those in genuine need rather than hoarding or indulging in "impulse buying" or luxury upgrades. It would prioritize the adoption of a lifestyle of simplicity, so as to mobilize more resources to support Christians in prison and distress in restricted nations. Such a community would confront the "world taken for granted" with a striking alternative and raise the possibility of critical examination, questioning, and ultimately rejection in favor of a more hopeful—and more God-centered—alternative. Here we come once again to the importance of Christian witness for John, as he calls forth a living

16. Peter L. Berger, *Invitation to Sociology: A Humanistic Perspective* (Doubleday, 1963), 110.

witness, a distinctive practice, that not only keeps our own souls clean from Babylon's defilements but also shakes the people around us out of thinking that "the way things are" is "the way things must be," inviting them to enter more closely into God's vision and purpose for human community.

Revelation thus invites us into serious dialogue with one another, with our Scriptures as a whole, and with our sisters and brothers across the world over such questions, so that we, too, may find ourselves "standing" before God and the Lamb at their coming. Wrestling together with these kinds of questions, I'm convinced, is one facet of what it means to engage Revelation seriously with a view to discovering what the Spirit is saying to the churches.

Reflection

In light of God's commands concerning and vision for human community, John calls for thoroughgoing evaluation of all of the systems of which we are a part and according to whose rules we play. Since this chapter has focused particularly on economics, your evaluation might begin there.

1. What are your own practices of earning, saving, and spending money? What values and beliefs do these practices reflect?
2. What is our society's "wisdom" (from financial advisors to advertising) regarding earning, saving, and spending?
3. What do the Torah, the prophets, Jesus, and the apostles say about earning, saving, and spending? Where do these teachings conflict with society's "wisdom" and your practices?
4. What would have to change in your practices to bring them more in line with God's values and desires for your use of resources? What obstacles, practical and ideological, stand in the way of doing so?
5. What will you do?

These questions can be adapted and repeated for any and every facet of your life and the practices of your society: gender roles, violence and war, lines of private and public, the "place" of religion, our relationship to and (ab)use of our environment, the values of self-gratification and self-fulfillment, and so on.

5

Encountering Christ in Revelation

We have been reading Revelation less as a coded text to be interpreted and more as a text that imposed a Christ-centered interpretation upon the everyday activities, landscapes, and stories encountered by the members of the seven congregations addressed by John in their setting. Having experienced the re-picturing of the cosmos as John's Apocalypse was read aloud to the gathered assembly, the hearers were changed, as was their everyday world, which they saw anew as but a part of a broader reality that put the everyday world into a different perspective. The voyeuristic experience of entering into John's encounter with the unseen world—and looking back from there upon the landscape of the visible world—provided a religious experience that disposed hearers indeed to "keep . . . the words of the prophecy of this book" (Rev. 22:7) as they returned to the normal world where they would hear the Christian prophetess "Jezebel" try to defend her position, encounter further propaganda about the emperor and *Dea Roma*, watch goods being transported to ports for transit by ship to Rome, try to engage in their business activities again, and encounter the other everyday realities of their cities. But these figures and activities would hardly look and feel the same, and the hearers would be raising far more critical questions as they moved through their lived experience in light of the "wider reality" (and its interpretation of their immediate realities) to which John had exposed them.

In this and the following chapter, we return to the opening segments of Revelation, first to look at where John directs his hearers' attention from the very outset. It was significant that John's visions began at the throne of God that God has shared with the Lamb, his Anointed One. It is also significant that the first figure to whom John introduces his readers in any detail is this Lamb, Jesus, the glorified Lord.

Look! He Is Coming with the Clouds!

The oracles addressed individually to the seven Christian communities in John's circuit reveal that these congregations were facing a number of challenges. Rival prophets were eroding the distinctive identity and witness of the group. Tension with the synagogue had escalated. Christian witness had elicited increasing suspicion and hostility in a number of cities. The spiritual health of particular congregations gave evidence of their decline. Beyond these issues, most of these Christian disciples would also have been concerned with more mundane challenges, like providing for their families, negotiating the world of business, or dealing with internal doubts concerning their allegiance to this minority group.

John effectively sets all of these more immediate challenges against the backdrop of a greater, overarching crisis that looms on the horizon. He does this so that his congregations will consider the more immediate challenges in light of this greater challenge, which will, in turn, incentivize particular responses to those more immediate challenges as the means by which to prepare for, and successfully meet, this greater crisis—the stakes of which are greatly elevated. This crisis is not the escalation of tension with the host society that John foresees (e.g., in Rev. 6:11b; 7:14b; 13:7, 15–17). That is merely a consequence of the continued faithfulness and witness to the one God and his Anointed One that John promotes. The crisis is not even the projected political and economic collapse of the empire. That is the result of God's just and necessary interventions in regard to an exploitative and violent regime. *The* critical challenge that must be given attention before all else is the forthcoming visitation of God and God's Messiah.

> John, to the seven churches that are in Asia: Grace and peace to you from the one who is and was and is coming, and from the seven spirits that are before God's throne, and from Jesus Christ—the faithful witness, the firstborn from among the dead, and the ruler of the kings of the earth. To the one who loves us and freed us from our sins by his blood, who made us a kingdom, priests to his God and Father—to him be glory and power forever and always. Amen. . . .
> "I am the Alpha and the Omega," says the Lord God, "the one who is and was and is coming, the Almighty." (Rev. 1:4–6, 8 CEB)

John describes God here at the outset not only as the "one who is and was," but also as "the one who is coming." The form of the Greek word that John has chosen here (*ho erchomenos*, 1:4, 8) speaks of God as one who is even now on his way, whose intervention in human affairs is imminent. Greeks and Romans used similar language to talk about the eternity of their chief deity, seen, once again, in the acclamation of Zeus: "Zeus was, Zeus is, Zeus shall be; O mighty Zeus!" (Pausanias, *Descr.* 10.12.10).[1] John makes a significant alteration in regard to the third clause. The picture is no longer of a God who exists forever in static eternity ("Zeus shall be"), but a God who will dynamically encounter God's creation. However much I personally love the hymn "Holy, Holy, Holy," based as it is on images and language from Revelation 4, the hymn writer got this wrong when he addressed God as the one "which wert and art and evermore shall be"—perhaps "which wert and art and comes victoriously" would better capture John's sense.

This dynamic encounter is more dramatically portrayed immediately following the greeting (1:4–6) in a clarion call to pay attention: "Look! He is coming with the clouds; every eye will see him, even those who pierced him, and all the tribes of the earth will wail on account of him" (1:7). John tells his churches to look ahead to an event of universal significance. He amplifies this coming crisis by drawing attention both to the breadth and trauma of its effects. It will evoke "wailing," a response reflecting unpreparedness and failure, and it will do so from "*all* the tribes of the earth." John further amplifies the crisis by drawing attention repeatedly to its imminence both at the outset and at the conclusion of his communication:

> For the time is near. (1:3)
> See, I am coming soon! (22:7)
> See, I am coming soon. (22:12)
> Surely I am coming soon. (22:20)

The greatest threat the hearers face is to be found unprepared to encounter God or God's Christ at his coming (6:12–17), thus being exposed to the horrors of the "second death" (2:11) or written out of the "book of life" (3:5). This challenge puts all the others in perspective, subordinates them to itself, and calls Christians to respond to their more immediate crises in the way that will also—and primarily—continue to position them well for encountering the returning Christ. As long as the disciples remained focused on the challenge of their neighbors' pressure, or the challenge of remaining on firm, economical footing, or any other of the everyday

1. Boring, Berger, and Colpe, eds., *Hellenistic Commentary*, 560.

challenges that they faced by virtue of being associated with the name of Jesus, they might move toward accommodating to the society around them, since that would generally resolve these challenges. John trumps all these rival foci by placing before the believers' eyes the ultimate crisis, the one most needing to be met successfully. In this way, John steers each disciple to choose the course of action in regard to those everyday challenges that will best align them with "the commandments of God and faithfulness toward Jesus" (14:12 AT).

But John also draws attention to an even more immediate "coming." One of the greatest surprises of Revelation is that the Lord for whom the disciples watch and wait already walks in the midst of his churches, inspecting, evaluating, preparing to prune away the unfruitful, unfaithful branches or to remove the lampstands whose light fails to burn as it ought. The image of Christ walking "among the seven gold lampstands" that represent the churches (2:1; see also 1:20) presents an even more immediate threat to congregations that have not kept faith with him.

And Christ now looks nothing like he did when he walked by the shores of the Sea of Galilee or through the streets of Jerusalem.

> I turned to see who was speaking to me, and when I turned, I saw seven oil lamps burning on top of seven gold stands. In the middle of the lampstands I saw someone who looked like the Son of Man.[2] He wore a robe that stretched down to his feet, and he had a gold sash around his chest. His head and hair were white as white wool—like snow—and his eyes were like a fiery flame. His feet were like fine brass that has been purified in a furnace, and his voice sounded like rushing water. He held seven stars in his right hand, and from his mouth came a sharp, two-edged sword. His appearance was like the sun shining with all its power. When I saw him, I fell at his feet like a dead man. But he put his right hand on me and said, "Don't be afraid. I'm the first and the last, and the living one. I was dead, but look! Now I'm alive forever and always. I have the keys of Death and the Grave." (1:12–18 CEB modified)

The Lord, now glorified beyond death, is far more powerful, awe-inspiring, and divine than even the most impressive alabaster statues of the Roman emperor, glowing in the smoky light of the oil lamps in the imperial temples, or than the most elaborate costumes and accessories could ever make the

2. The CEB reads "the Human One" in the main text and offers "Son of Man" as an alternative reading in a textual note. The rendering "Human One" for "Son of Man," however, is likely the most controversial translational decision made by the editors of the CEB.

living emperor appear. Unless the congregations fall in line swiftly with the glorified Christ's righteous demands (for example, recovering their former love and their former commitment to avoid every semblance of idolatrous worship, 2:4, 15, 20), Christ's immediacy threatens swift judgment with no need to wait for the second coming:

> I will come to you and remove your lampstand from its place, unless you repent. (2:5)
>
> Repent, then. If not, I will come to you soon and wage war against them with the sword of my mouth. (2:16)
>
> I am throwing her on a bed, and those who commit adultery with her I am throwing into great distress, unless they repent of her doings; and I will strike her children dead. And all the churches will know that I am the one who searches minds and hearts, and I will give to each of you as your works deserve. (2:22–23)

At the same time, however, if one is disposed to heed Jesus's summons, his presence in the midst of the churches signifies the immediacy of help and fellowship.

The oracle to Laodicea, appropriately the last of the series of seven, closes the distance between the congregations and their imminently expected lord even further. The one who throughout the oracles declared that he is coming appears now to have arrived at the very threshold: "Look! I'm standing at the door and knocking" (3:20 CEB). Christians must come to terms at once, then, with the glorified Christ who stands at the door, whether for judgment or strengthening. John guides the churches to see that their response to Christ's exhortations to single-hearted discipleship will determine whether they encounter him on the other side of this door as judge and executioner, or as a welcome guest.

It is not difficult to discern what John would say to us through the opening chapter of his Revelation, for it remains essentially the same as his challenge to his own congregations.

If, with John, we keep the day of the wrath of God and of the Lamb (6:16–17; see also 1:7) before our eyes, what we must decide to do this day, and how we must respond to each new presenting situation, becomes that much clearer.

If, with John, we know Jesus as "the ruler of the kings of the earth" and as the "one who loves us and freed us from our sins by his blood, who made us a kingdom, priests serving his God and Father" (1:5–6), our primary identity will be rooted in our place in the kingdom of God, which we share with the redeemed from every people, tribe, nation, and language group. It will not be rooted in some national or political body constructed by human beings and their party lines. Our primary allegiance will be to this one Lord and one God in every aspect of our lives, out of gratitude for our costly redemption and in acknowledgment that we have been made part of a very real political entity whose head is Christ.

If, with John, we know Jesus not as he was when he walked the roads of Palestine, but as he is now that he has entered into a transformed existence beyond all mortal experience, we will know the awesome majesty of the One whom we worship, and in whose name we go forth to serve as "priests" (1:6; 5:10). This will give us courage, as it gave John and as John hoped it would give his congregations, to confront abusive and exploitative practices in families, businesses, and governments, to relieve the needs of the suffering, and to bear witness to God's way of ordering a just and humane society. And we will do these things, not in fear of the overshadowing powers of the enemy, but in confidence in the triumph of the Christ who sits at God's right hand, invested with God's power, and who is coming to bring justice to "every tribe, language, people, and nation" (5:9; see also 7:9; 13:7; 14:6). He who is the beginning and the ending will always have the last word over all who oppose God's righteous reign.

And John would also have us, as we prepare to meet him at his coming, alert to find the glorified Christ already standing in the midst of his churches affirming our works of faith, confronting our compromise, and encouraging our renewed devotion. Thus John calls us to be prepared to encounter Jesus as he walks in our midst, and to be mindful of the urgency of responding to what this Jesus would tell us, since by means of such response we might indeed avoid being left in a position to wail at his return.

The Jesus Whom John Proclaims

Notable voices have expressed a low regard for John's presentation of Jesus in Revelation. In the earlier years of the Reformation, Martin Luther asserted that the book hardly deserved its place in the Christian canon because "Christ is not taught or known in it; but to teach Christ is the thing which an apostle above all else is to do."[3] Four centuries later, the novelist D. H. Lawrence, while finding Christ in Revelation, expressed extreme disapproval of the Christ that he found:

> Always the titles of power, and never the titles of love. Always Christ the omnipotent conqueror flashing his great sword and destroying, destroying vast masses of men, till blood mounts up to the horses' bridles. Never Christ the Saviour: never.[4]

An unprejudiced examination of Revelation must lead one to disagree with such sentiments.

As we have seen, John has brought the glorified Christ before his readers by the end of the first chapter, describing him in terms that connect him both to the "Ancient of Days" and to the "one like a son of man" in Daniel 7 (see especially the language of Dan. 7:9, 13 [ESV]; Rev. 1:13–14) and thus as the one to whom royal dominion would be given forever, ending the rule of the more bestial empires whose line has filled human history (Dan. 7:14, 27). This "ruler of the kings of the earth" is also "the one who loves us and freed us from our sins by his blood" (Rev. 1:5)—"Christ the Saviour," indeed, against Lawrence's claim—"and made us a kingdom, priests serving his God and Father" (1:6).

Jesus's redemptive offering of himself appears again in the scenes around the throne of God in Revelation 5: "You were slaughtered and by your blood you ransomed for God saints from every tribe and language and people and nation; you have made them a kingdom and priests serving our God" (5:9–10). While John affirms release from sins (1:5), the more traditional consequence of Jesus's self-giving death, the accent of Jesus's redemptive work in Revelation falls on the establishment of this alternative kingdom and the "ransoming" of people from every temporal demographic grouping for this alternative kingdom, co-ruled by "the One seated on the throne" and "the Lamb" (5:13) into the ages of ages.[5]

John's angelic conversation partner in this scene asserts that, in this manner, "the Lion from the tribe of Judah, the Root of David, conquered,"

3. 1522 Preface to the New Testament, quoted in Judith Kovacs and Christopher Rowland, *Revelation: The Apocalypse of Jesus Christ* (Blackwell, 2004), 44.

4. D. H. Lawrence, *Apocalypse* (Knopf, 1931), 34.

5. So also J. Nelson Kraybill, *Apocalypse and Allegiance: Worship, Politics, and Devotion in the Book of Revelation* (Brazos, 2010), 101.

with the result that he can take possession of the scroll in God's hand, open its seals, and begin to unroll history itself to its final denouement (5:5). Scholars often make much of the fact that John *hears* this announcement concerning a "Lion"—identifying Jesus with language that clearly marks him out as the Davidic Messiah (see Gen. 49:9; Isa. 11:1, 10)—but *sees* a Lamb, standing despite having obviously been slaughtered. By the time John writes, and given that some of his audience, at least, would be quite mature believers, this transition from "Lion" to "Lamb" would not have taken his hearers by surprise. When they joined themselves to this movement, they understood that they were committing themselves to an anointed agent of God who achieved God's purposes not through violent revolution but by not loving his life to the point of death, even as his followers would need to commit themselves to do (12:11; see also 2:8, 10; 11:7–13; 15:2–4). This manner of conquering is surely significant, calling into question the degree to which the Christ of Revelation can be called an "omnipotent conqueror flashing his great sword," as if his manner of conquering were indeed violent or his sword anything more than the word of his testimony and the power it carries (1:16; 19:15). Though slaughtered, the Lamb is not sheepish. His seven horns symbolize the power and authority that God has delegated to him. His seven eyes ascribe to him the all-seeing gaze of God himself, an all-encompassing view that John invokes as an incentive to faithful practice in every situation (as in 2:23). And his coming in judgment evokes abject terror on the part even of this world's rulers and military commanders (6:15–17).

John portrays Jesus as exhibiting ongoing care for and consistent solidarity with his followers. In the vision of Revelation 7:9–17, the redeemed from "every nation, from all tribes and peoples and languages" stand before God and the Lamb, having passed through great trial, acclaiming God and the Lamb for their deliverance (7:9, 14). The vision closes with the tender scene: "The Lamb who is in the midst of the throne will shepherd them. He will lead them to the springs of life-giving water, and God will wipe away every tear from their eyes" (7:17 CEB). The image may recall the activity of the divine shepherd in Psalm 23, who similarly leads the devotee "beside still waters," as well as the ruler promised by Ezekiel who, unlike the self-serving rulers under which God's people had endured exploitation and oppression, would shepherd them with faithfulness and genuine investment in their well-being (Ezek. 34:23–31).

The Lamb is not only present with his faithful after their contest but in the midst of it as well. John sees those who had been sealed for God

(7:3–8) once again in his visions, this time immediately after his narration of the onslaught that the dragon has orchestrated and let loose against them (12:17–13:18): "And I looked, and there was the Lamb standing on Mount Zion! And with him were one hundred forty-four thousand who had his name and his Father's name written on their foreheads. . . . These follow the Lamb wherever he goes" (14:1, 4). John sees Jesus thus standing in solidarity with those who must now face the contest that he had faced—and must conquer very much as he did, not loving their lives to the point of dying (12:11)—loving faithful obedience to God's commandments and the testimony of Jesus more (12:17).

Jesus appears prominently again in a two-part scene that anticipates the last judgment:

> And I looked, and behold! A white cloud, and seated on the cloud was one like a son of man, having a gold wreath upon his head and a sharp sickle in his hand. And another angel came out from the temple shouting in a loud voice to the one seated upon the cloud: "Put in your sickle and reap, because the hour of harvest has come, because the harvest of the earth has become ripe." And the one seated upon the cloud cast his sickle into the earth and the earth was harvested.
>
> And another angel came out from the temple that is in heaven having himself a sharp sickle. And another angel came out from the altar, who had authority over fire, and he spoke in a great voice to the one having the sharp sickle, saying: "Put in your sharp sickle and harvest the clusters of the vine of the earth, for its grapes have become ripe." And the angel cast his sickle into the earth and harvested the vine of the earth and cast them into the great winepress of the wrath of God. And the winepress was trodden outside the city and blood went forth from the winepress as high as the bridles of horses for a distance of 1,600 stadia. (14:14–20 AT)

The first scene in the pair presents a reaping of earth's harvest, and there is good reason to regard this as a salvific gathering of those who belong to God and to Jesus; the second scene is unmistakably a representation of condemnation. Jesus was himself remembered to have spoken of the judgment at the end of the age as involving a gathering of the faithful and the disposal of the unrighteous (Matt. 13:24–30, 37–43). Familiarity with this tradition would dispose hearers of Revelation 14:14–20 to interpret the two scenes in this way. Earlier, John presented the 144,000 as "first fruits for God" (14:4) which also sets up an expectation for a full harvest of the redeemed, such as is depicted here. The fate of those gathered in the second harvest—to be trampled in the winepress of God's wrath—leaves no room for doubt that this is an undesirable outcome. The "one like the Son of Man" (14:14), an echo of John's presentation of Jesus in 1:13 but also a phrase closely associated with God's messiah in general and with Jesus in particular, is associated here with the positive ingathering. The paired scenes of judgment here, breaking into the narrative action of Revelation out of sequence, continue to hold before John's audiences the principal challenge facing them, in light of which they must strategically choose how they will respond to the more immediate but secondary challenges facing them in their local contexts. The scenes of judgment also serve to remind the audiences that their final and eternal destiny is for Jesus to determine, such that allegiance to him in the here and now will always prove more advantageous in the long run.

Perhaps the most celebrated appearance of Jesus in Revelation's unfolding drama occurs after the judgment of Babylon and prior to the denouement of the present age, when he returns at the head of the hosts of heaven to do battle with the beast and his allied forces:

> And I saw heaven opened, and look! A white horse, and the one seated upon it called "Faithful" and "True," and he judges and makes war justly. His eyes were as a flame of fire and upon his head were many diadems. He had a name written which no one knows except he himself, and he was clad about with a garment dipped in blood, and his name has been called "the Word of God." And the armies in heaven, clad in clean, white linen, were following him upon white horses. And from his mouth proceeds a sharp sword, in order that he might strike the nations and he himself shepherd them with an iron rod. And he himself will tread the winepress of the fury of the wrath of God *Pantokratōr* [the Almighty one]. And he has a name inscribed on his garment and on his thigh: King of kings and Lord of lords. (19:11–16 AT)

John gives his hearers every reason to connect this figure with the glorified Jesus. The eyes (compare 1:14; 2:18), the sword proceeding from the mouth (compare 1:16; 2:12), and the title (compare "Lord of lords and King of kings" in 17:14) all point in that direction, as do the references to typical messianic texts (e.g., ruling the nations with an iron rod; see Ps. 2:9). The Lamb who ransoms is also the champion who vindicates, imposing judgment on those who have advanced Satan's work of leading the nations astray and who have trampled the faithful followers of the one God and the Lamb.

The detail that he wears a garment that has been dipped in blood commands attention. It is tempting to identify this with the blood of Jesus's enemies, particularly if we recall the scene in Revelation 14:17–20 and think of the figure in Isaiah 63:1–6 who returns from wreaking vengeance on Edom (the nation to the immediate south of Judah) with his garments stained with blood—from having "trodden the winepress . . . in my anger" (63:3). But the scenes in Revelation 14:14–20 are a forecast of the last judgment, and Jesus is presented even here as the one who "*will* tread the winepress of the fury of the wrath of God the Almighty" (19:15). He has not done so yet. Those interpreters are probably correct who see here a reference to (and thus a reminder of) the blood that Jesus himself had spilled on behalf of those he ransomed, riding now to vindicate them against those who have aligned themselves with the enemies of God and God's people.

The battle scene here seems to pick up the narrative thread from where the sixth libation bowl left the hearers, with the beast's and false prophet's armies gathered for a battle that does not occur until now (16:12–16). For all the hype that "Armageddon" (16:16 ESV) receives in popular culture, John's battle of Armageddon is nothing even close to a contest. Indeed, it seems to be over as soon as it is joined. The beast and his false prophet are plucked up and cast unceremoniously into the lake of fire while their assembled armies are dispatched with the sword that proceeds from the mouth of the glorified Christ, leaving their bodies to be a feast for the birds of the air (19:17–21, with echoes of Ezek. 39:17–20). This effortless victory cannot fail to evoke confidence among John's congregations, displaying before them the far greater power and authority of the Lord to whom they have given their allegiance, and thereby continuing to strengthen their commitment to continue in that allegiance.

We see Christ in two more scenes in John's vision, the first being the millennial reign of the faithful, who "came to life and reigned with Christ a thousand years," who "will be priests of God and of Christ, and will reign with him a thousand years" (20:4, 6). These faithful are described as "the souls of those who had been axed on account of the testimony of Jesus and on account of the word of God, and whoever did not worship the beast or its image and did not receive the mark upon their forehead and upon their right hand" (20:4 AT). John here promises the enjoyment of a tremendous privilege to those among his congregations who love "not their lives even unto death" (12:11 ESV) and who heed his summons to abstain from all forms of imperial cult. First, they enjoy a period of exaltation with their Lord out of all proportion to the time of their trials on his behalf. This is the fruition of his promise to share his throne and authority with those who overcome even as God shared his throne and authority with Jesus (3:21). Second, they enjoy the assurance that they stand in no danger of the "second death," the lake of fire that is the destiny of those who have failed to fear God and honor his commandments (20:6). The second of these scenes is, of course, the life of the new Jerusalem, wherein God and the Lamb, who are fully present with the ransomed multitude, are the very light that radiates throughout the redeemed community (21:23; 22:3–4). In all the scenes of the redeemed, a chief component of the privilege they enjoy is their intimate communion with God and with Jesus forever—in Paul's words, "and thus we will always be with the Lord" (1 Thess. 4:17 AT).

John avoids making explicit statements concerning the relationship of Jesus, the Messiah, to the one eternal God. He does, however, provide a great deal of material that readily lends itself to the conviction, increasingly embraced throughout the early church, that Jesus shared in some mystical way in the eternity of God. God is identified as "the Alpha and the Omega" (the first and last letters of the Greek alphabet) at the outset of Revelation (1:8), while Jesus introduces himself in very similar terms as "the First and the Last" (1:17; see also 2:8), using language heard from God's mouth in Isaiah: "I am the first, and I am the last; besides me there is no god" (Isa. 44:6). God identifies himself again in the verses introducing the new heavens and new earth as "the Alpha and the Omega, the Beginning and the End" (Rev. 21:6). In the closing sentences of Revelation, *Jesus* declares: "*I* am the Alpha and the Omega, the First and the Last, the Beginning and the End" (22:13). John signals his own conviction thereby that the One seated upon the throne and his Anointed One share essential characteristics, most prominently eternity of being, that elevate the latter to the level of deity. It is no doubt because of this close identification of God and "the Lamb" that the latter can rightfully receive worship throughout the scenes of Revelation in a theological setting in which only God is worthy of worship (as affirmed by "the commandments of God" to which John points repeatedly).

A Genuine Revelation of Jesus Christ

Against Luther's premature judgment of Revelation as offering the disciple little of Jesus, Jean-Pierre Prévost's observation appears to be the more correct one:

> If we read [Revelation] to discover something about Jesus Christ, we shall be served royally. Do it for that reason alone, to reveal the riches of the person of

> Christ and the significance of the events of his death and resurrection for the future of the world.[6]

John's proclamation of Jesus resonates deeply with the "mystery of faith" confessed by liturgically oriented churches across the globe, namely: "Christ has died. Christ is risen. Christ will come again." John solemnly commemorates Jesus's death on behalf of people from every nation, tribe, and language, releasing them from their sin (and its consequences), ransoming them to become God's own people, the kingdom that the "one like the Son of Man" (Rev. 1:13; 14:14) has been given by God (1:5–6; 5:9–10). John also proclaims Christ risen, "the firstborn of the dead" (1:5). Christ says, "I am . . . the Living One. I was dead, and see, I am alive forever and ever, and I have the keys of Death and of Hades" (1:17–18; see also 2:8). In concert with other voices, John proclaims that Jesus's own triumph over death gives him authority over death, so that he has the power to give life again to his faithful ones and even to bring about the final destruction of death itself (20:14; 21:4). And from beginning to end, John reminds his hearers that Christ *will* come again to gather his faithful ones and to execute judgment upon the faithless who have given their allegiance to the powers that oppose God's redemptive work in the world: "See, I am coming soon; my reward is with me, to repay according to everyone's work" (22:12); "The one who testifies to these things says, 'Surely I am coming soon.' Amen. Come, Lord Jesus!" (22:20).

Reflection

1. What are the images of Jesus that you typically carry around with you or visualize in prayer or worship?
2. How does John challenge you to expand your repertoire of images?
3. How does John's "revelation of Jesus Christ" contribute to your understanding of Jesus's character and place in the ongoing unfolding of God's plan for his cosmos?

6. Jean-Pierre Prévost, *How to Read the Apocalypse* (Crossroad, 1993), 3.

6

What the Spirit Says to the Churches: The Seven Oracles

The seven oracles to the seven churches are among the more frequently preached-upon passages in Revelation and therefore among the more familiar. I say "oracles," again, rather than "letters," because each communication to a congregation begins with a variant of the prophetic oracle formula "Thus says the Lord," as in "These things says the One who holds the seven stars" (Rev. 2:1 AT). The formula that precedes the content of each of these oracles—"To the angel of the church . . . write"—would not be heard as a variation of the letter-opening formula, but rather as a command to John, the visionary prophet, to record the prophetic speech (the "oracle") of the glorified Lord that follows. These oracles are favorite texts for preaching since pastors rightly intuit that reflecting on what Jesus commended and censured in these churches can help us diagnose what Jesus would commend and censure in our churches.

The seven oracles follow a formulaic pattern, with only minor variations:

1. Jesus identifies himself as the one speaking, usually reminding the congregation of some significant facet of his identity, power, or achievement.
2. Jesus identifies what the particular congregation being addressed has been doing well, and he encourages and honors them for this.
3. Jesus identifies where the congregation, or some portion thereof, has fallen short of a discerning, wholehearted response of faithfulness, and challenges them to give their attention and energies to remedying these deficiencies.
4. Jesus warns the congregation of the consequences of failing to invest themselves in constructive change in these areas and encourages

them with the positive consequences of taking his diagnosis and admonitions to heart.

5. The hearers are solemnly admonished to "hear what the Spirit is saying to the congregations" (2:7 AT; so also 2:11, 17, 28; 3:6, 13, 22).

John gives a number of clues that he expects his hearers to meditate on these prophetic oracles to their congregations in light of the whole of Revelation—reinforcing, incidentally, the primary thesis that Revelation as a whole, and not just these opening oracles, was written with these first-century congregations in mind (rather than us). For example, while the images Jesus uses to identify himself are almost all drawn from John's initial vision of Jesus in chapter 1, many of the warnings and promises involve images that are only explained later in the visions. The "tree of life that is in the paradise of God" (2:7), the threat of the "second death" (2:11), the promise of "the morning star" (2:28), Jesus making war "with the sword of [his] mouth" (2:16), the significance of the "book of life" and being "clothed . . . in white robes" (3:5), being inscribed with the name of "the new Jerusalem that comes down from my God" (3:12), and sharing Jesus's authority upon thrones (3:21) all look ahead to the actions and scenes of Revelation 7 and 19–22.[1] As we examine a selection of these oracles, then, we will also be attentive to how the material in Revelation that precedes and follows them illumines and reinforces their contents. We will also be attentive to how the members of each church would have deepened their reading of their own situation as they moved from hearing the oracle that specifically addresses them to processing the whole of Revelation, with the visions of chapters 4–22 continuing to shape their perception of their landscape, its challenges, and the response that would prove most advantageous in the long run.

Smyrna

Write this to the angel of the church in Smyrna:

"These are the words of the one who is the first and the last, who died and came back to life: I know your hardship and poverty (though you are actually rich). I also know the hurtful things that have been spoken about you by those

1. The "tree of life" (22:2, 14); the "second death" (20:6, 14–15; 21:8); the "morning star" (22:16); white robes (7:9–14); names inscribed in the book of life (20:11–12, 15; 21:27); sharing Jesus's rule (20:4–6; 22:5); the "new Jerusalem" (21:1–22:5 as a whole).

> who say they are Jews (though they are not, but are really Satan's synagogue). Don't be afraid of what you are going to suffer. Look! The devil is going to throw some of you into prison in order to test you. You will suffer hardship for ten days. Be faithful even to the point of death, and I will give you the crown of life. If you can hear, listen to what the Spirit is saying to the churches. Those who emerge victorious won't be hurt by the second death." (2:8–11 CEB)

Breaking the general pattern of the oracles, there is no word of rebuke for this congregation. The church whose situation is the most miserable is most honored in Christ's eyes!

The oracle identifies three important issues in the life of this congregation: first, their material poverty; second, the hostility between the church and the local synagogue; and third, the likelihood of social pressure escalating to martyrdom in the near future. The cause of the Christians' poverty in this city is not made explicit, but we do know that John is intensely concerned that Christians should not profit from the Roman imperial economy, since he regards the system itself as an entangling web of injustice and exploitation that will drag its partners down with it under God's judgment. The Smyrnaean Christians appear to have avoided such entanglements. But we might surmise further that their poverty comes from their refusal to do what it takes to maintain business networks in a pagan city, and from their neighbors' increasing alienation from them because of their changed lifestyle. Economic embargo could be a powerful, unofficial tool to let deviants know you don't approve of their new behaviors. Thus their temporal poverty may well be a consequence of their obedience to God's call, and this loyal obedience has otherwise made them rich in Christ's estimation.

The issue of the level of persecution facing this congregation and the other churches is an important one, all the more as most every thumbnail sketch of the setting of Revelation claims that John was writing to comfort churches that are suffering severe persecution. A close look at the whole of Revelation suggests that we need a much more nuanced view. It is certainly true that the non-Christians were suspicious of, and often hostile to, the early Christian movement. The kinds of harassment that some of the Christians addressed by John were experiencing might have been limited to verbal assaults ("slander," 2:9), economic hardship ("poverty," 2:9), and other indignities they were "enduring" (2:3; see also v. 19). Insults, physical abuse, and disenfranchisement were the common lot of many Christians throughout the eastern Mediterranean (see Heb. 10:32–34; 13:3; 1 Pet. 2:11–12, 18–25; 3:13–17; 4:1–4, 12–19; 1 Thess. 3:1–6; 2 Thess. 1:3–9).

Such harassment communicated a message: The Christians' neighbors were calling this deviant minority group to fall in line again with the values and behaviors considered important for the larger society's well-being. Their neighbors would have been particularly keen on motivating them to return to the traditional piety upon which all other social values were founded, and to the solidarity and civic unity that such piety expressed and facilitated. This call, no doubt, weighed heavily on the minds of many Christians, pushing them to think about how to balance the human drive to enjoy a serene and secure life with their religious commitments to the God of Israel and his Messiah. This is especially evident in the Christian communities in Pergamum and Thyatira (see below). John also knew that continued resistance to their neighbors' summons would eventuate in heavier-handed attempts on society's part to address the problem of deviants in their midst, filling up the tally of the martyrs (6:11). John had no illusions about the consequences of his preferred course of action.

Martyrdom, however, was in fact quite rare in the first century. It usually affected leaders rather than the general membership. Rome appears not to have gone looking for Christians to prosecute, even in the early second century. It was local rather than empire-wide. Even when Nero scapegoated the Christians in Rome for the great fire in 64 CE, Nero's actions were limited to the Roman Christian community in connection with a specific crime—arson—and did not become a precedent for the treatment of Christians. While John remembers that those and other Christians had died under Roman rule, seen, for example, in the episode of the souls of Jesus's witnesses crying out from under the altar for vindication (6:9–11), John names only one near-contemporary martyr from the seven churches—Antipas of Pergamum (2:13). And we know nothing of the circumstances of his death, whether it was the result of official proceedings or a back-alley lynching. There is also no Roman record of Domitian's having taken any actions against Christians throughout the empire, though he was responsible for executing several high-ranking Roman converts in the capital itself on the charge of "atheism" (whether as converts to a more traditional Judaism or to the Christian movement is unclear).

Even more problematic for John are those congregations that seem to coexist all too peaceably with their neighbors in the shadow of Rome. There is not a hint that the Christians in Sardis and Laodicea have experienced rejection by their neighbors. Indeed, the indictment of these churches appears to stem from the fact that they blend in all too well and mingle all too effectively with the partners of Rome and worshipers of idols all around them. As we think about the diversity of the congregations John addresses, we should always bear in mind that John is equally interested in comforting the afflicted and afflicting the comfortable.

John does see in Antipas, however, the shape of things to come if Christians continue in their bold witness as did Antipas. His violent death shows Christians just how precarious their position is and why muting their Christian witness rather than trumpeting their allegiance to Jesus might be the more prudent course. Such witness criticized the heart of the empire and could not help but provoke a strong, allergic response among those who, as partners of "Babylon," looked to that empire for security and even prosperity. The vignette of the two witnesses in Revelation 11:3–13—which may serve more as an inspiration to John's audience to take on the role of "witness" boldly rather than as a prediction of some particular pair who will rise up—reinforces the pattern. Though enjoying God's protection and God's reinforcement of their witness through manifestations of God's power, the witnesses nevertheless suffer violent deaths and further degradation as their corpses lie unburied in the street. It is only after their faithfulness unto death that change would come to the hearts of "the inhabitants of the earth" (11:10). Though vindication through resurrection is promised, witnessing to the point of death would remain an act of faith that, in John's vision at least, only reaps positive results among the unbelieving population postmortem.

The scenes of marginalization and martyrdom that dominate the visions are mostly visions for the near future, not of John's present, and history proved John to be correct. Perhaps in as few as twenty years after John's Revelation circulated among the churches in Roman Asia, Christians in the neighboring province of Bithynia would be faced with a choice eerily reminiscent of the scenes in Revelation 13:12, 16–17. Pliny the Younger was governor of Bithynia in 112–113 CE. Many of his letters survive, among them 121 letters he exchanged with the emperor Trajan during his year as governor. In one of those letters, Pliny writes to seek guidance or confirmation concerning the procedures he has followed in regard to a significant number of people who have been denounced before him as being "Christians" (*Epistle* 10.96). He admits that he had little prior knowledge of what "being a Christian" entailed, so he examined under torture two female slaves (who, he learned, were "deaconesses" in the movement) to fill in the gaps. He knew enough, however, to regard identifying oneself as a Christian to be a punishable offense, particularly since Christians were known to refuse to sacrifice to the empire's gods and to the emperor himself. If the accused admitted to being "Christians" after being given three chances to renounce the title, Pliny sentenced them to be executed—for their stubbornness in not recanting, if nothing else. Those who denied that they were Christians were given the opportunity to invoke the traditional gods and to offer wine and incense before the emperor Trajan's statue as proof of their loyalty and to curse the name of Christ. Pliny essentially congratulated himself for offering pardon to those who had been Christians but said they had since left the group, since leaving a path open to rehabilitation had allowed him to spare a good number of people and had had the effect of reviving attention more broadly to traditional religious rites. In his reply (*Epistle* 10.97), Trajan affirmed Pliny in this policy: Those who showed proper piety to the gods when thus confronted would be pardoned. This is the sort of forthcoming trial that John announces for the Christians in Smyrna and for which he seeks to prepare all his congregations.

The description of Smyrna's Jewish community in Revelation shows us that hostility between church and synagogue went both ways. When the glorified Christ calls them "a synagogue of Satan" (Rev. 2:9; 3:9), he is engaging in the same kind of name-calling we find in other situations where closely related groups have arguments with one another. In the Fourth Gospel, Jesus denounces opposing Jewish leaders as the spawn of Satan (John 8:44), and the members of the Jewish sect at Qumran referred to other Jews outside their group as the "congregation of Beliar" (1QH 2:22; 1QM 4:9). But the label "synagogue of Satan" may reflect more than a stock slur. In Revelation, Satan is the force behind the principate and the imperial cult. The worship and authority of the emperor is grounded in the worship and authority of Satan. When John's audience looks for Satan, the leader of the demonic forces, in their context, John leads them to look toward Zeus—the leader of their neighbors' "gods" and the divine force supporting the rule of Rome through her emperors according to the dominant cultural ideology.

The Jewish people were generally careful to observe the first commandment and avoid any entanglements with idolatrous cults. A recent development in their history, however, may have won John's enduring censure. The Jews had formerly expressed their loyalty to the emperors by offering sacrifices in their temple in Jerusalem on the emperor's behalf. This exempted Jews throughout the empire from having to demonstrate their loyalty by participating in local sacrifices *to* the emperor. After the temple's destruction in 70 CE, however, a new sign of loyalty was imposed upon Judeans. Adult male Jews had long been contributing two denarii each to the temple every year to help support the daily sacrifices and the ongoing maintenance of the premises. Vespasian (ruled 69–79 CE) ordered that this "temple tax" would continue to be collected and would be collected from that point on from both adult men and women, and the proceeds sent to Rome. These were used at first to underwrite the cost of rebuilding the Temple of Jupiter Capitolinus, which had been burned down during the civil war of 68–69, and then to continue to support its cult and maintenance (Josephus, *J. W.* 7.6.6, §218). The price of toleration thus became an annual contribution to a pagan cult—indeed, the principal pagan cult in the city of Rome—literally taking what belonged to God and giving it to Caesar and *his* god. This practice allowed local Jewish communities to continue to flourish in the Roman economy and enjoy legal toleration within the empire. It might have seemed a reasonable compromise, and indeed a sign of Rome's leniency after the Jewish Revolt. But, for the impractical and uncompromising prophet on Patmos, his fellow Jews had compromised their witness and loyalty to the one God by their willingness to give the tribute due to the one true God to the central religious site of the Roman anti-God, putting them in league with Satan.

Above, FIGURE 6.1. Denarius of Titus (emperor 79–81 CE). The reverse features the facade of the Temple of Jupiter on the Capitoline Hill in Rome. The coin celebrates the renovation of this historic worship site. (Courtesy of Classical Numismatic Group, LLC; www.CNG-coins.com.) See page 171 for color version.

Below, FIGURE 6.2. A Tyrian shekel minted 107 BCE. This was the currency in which the temple tax had historically been paid, the tax that was diverted after 70 CE to subvent the costs of the restoration and operation of the Temple of Jupiter in Rome. (Courtesy of Robert Deutsch, Archaeological Center, Jaffa; auction 48, lot 17; www.archaeological-center.com.)

What John describes as the synagogue's "slander" of the Christians is also intelligible against the backdrop of Jewish communities living in the shadows cast by the failed Jewish Revolt of 66–70 CE. Christian claims about the meaning of the Jewish Scriptures, the identity of the people of God, and the role of the Torah in the people of God were problematic for other Jews from the beginning. After the suppression of the First Jewish Revolt, however, Jews would be even more interested in distancing themselves from a group whose leader had been crucified as a revolutionary, a group whose members eagerly awaited his return to finish what he started. Monitoring boundaries closely, pointing out that Christians were not Jews, would help maintain good relations with both Roman officials and their own business associates. By dissociating themselves from the Christians, however, the synagogue would potentially set in motion investigations on the part of Rome's agents that would expose the Christian disciples as a potentially subversive group that, when examined, would be subjected to penal action, since it was becoming clear that the Christian movement did not enjoy the official toleration and exemptions afforded to Jews.

John prepares the believers in Smyrna for a coming sifting. Some of them will be examined, imprisoned, and executed. In the Roman system, imprisonment was not a form of punishment. Rather, it was used to detain defendants awaiting trial, to gain the cooperation of recalcitrant parties, and to hold till their execution those sentenced to death, hence the call to "be faithful even to the point of death" (2:10) in this situation.

The Smyrnaean Christians will find much in the later visions that resonates with their situation. The official proceedings they are about to face are one instance of Satan's determination to make war with the sisters and brothers of the divine child who was caught up into heaven—namely, Jesus himself (12:17). Satan would wage this war through the instruments of Roman power and jurisprudence that he summoned (13:1–18). The local trials they faced were but one manifestation of an empire-wide trial facing the entire brotherhood and sisterhood. They would be encouraged in the face of their material poverty as they considered the corruption and defilement that permeated the economy of Babylon (Rev. 18). They would see themselves in the companies of victors who overcame Satan's trials, who wear the wreaths of victory promised to those who remained faithful unto death (2:10; 7:13–17; 15:1–4; 20:4–6). They would see the "second death" that threatened all who compromised their faithfulness to the one God, from which Jesus promised they would be forever safe after their steadfastness (2:11; 14:9–11; 20:11–15). Of course, they also had the assurance of Jesus's own example, who had himself shown the way to overcome by displaying fidelity unto death, and was indeed living proof that death was only the beginning (2:8).

Pergamum and Thyatira

> Write this to the angel of the church in Pergamum:
>
> "These are the words of the one who has the sharp, two-edged sword: I know that you are living right where Satan's throne is. You are holding on to my name, and you didn't break faith with me even at the time that Antipas, my faithful witness, was killed among you, where Satan lives. But I have a few things against you, because you have some there who follow Balaam's teaching. Balaam had taught Balak to trip up the Israelites so that they would eat food sacrificed to idols and commit sexual immorality. In the same way, you have some who follow the Nicolaitans' teaching. So change your hearts and lives. If you don't, I am coming to you soon, and I will make war on them with the sword that comes from my mouth. If you can hear, listen to what the Spirit is saying to the churches. I will give those who emerge victorious some of the hidden manna to eat. I will also give to each of them a white stone with a new name written on it, which no one knows except the one who receives it." (2:12–17 CEB)

We have already addressed the issue of the hostility of the Pergamene Christians' neighbors and the death of Antipas, the lone-named martyr from the seven churches. The major issue facing this congregation concerns the "gospel" of the Nicolaitans. This accommodationist teaching is also the major issue John raises in the congregation in Thyatira, where a particular Christian prophetess also preaches a problematic gospel:

> I have this against you: you put up with that woman, Jezebel, who calls herself a prophet. You allow her to teach and to mislead my servants into committing sexual immorality and eating food sacrificed to idols. I gave her time to change her heart and life, but she refuses to change her life of prostitution. Look! I'm throwing her onto a sickbed. I am casting those who have committed adultery with her into terrible hardship—if they don't change their hearts from following her practices—and I will even put her children to death with disease. (2:20–23 CEB)

All that John tells us about these rival teachers in both cities is that they lead Christians "to eat things sacrificed to idols and to have illicit sexual relations"

(2:14–15 AT; so also in v. 20). Whatever this may mean, this much is clear: The rival teachers try to make room for Christians to interact more closely with their non-Christian neighbors where pagan rites are concerned.

Where would people eat food sacrificed to idols, and why would an inner-Christian movement seek to render such action defensible? Public religious festivals were frequently occasions for social feasting, opportunities to celebrate the solidarity enjoyed between citizenry and gods. One would also encounter "food sacrificed to idols" at private dinner parties or at dinners of clubs and associations (including those centered on a common trade or industry), which involved rites paying honor to the patron god or goddess and, increasingly, to the emperor as an antidote to any suspicion against such clubs. Trade associations, while not serving the same functions as unions today, nevertheless provided important opportunities for networking, offered a stable circle of social relationships, and often formed something of a safety net in times of hardship, as when an association would provide for the proper burial of members when their families could not afford it.

The person who sought to avoid any idolatrous rite and any food that had been "consecrated" by such a rite would have to withdraw from a great many important social and business settings, with serious social and economic consequences. The "Nicolaitans" and "Jezebel" were promoting an understanding of Christian practice that would allow Christians to participate in those social, civic, and perhaps even religious contexts where food sacrificed to idols would be ingested. Such flexibility would alleviate a great deal of social tension between church and society and open up the doors once again to those networks that facilitated survival or even thriving.

John doesn't tell us how Jezebel or the Nicolaitans argued their case, but neither was this the first time Christians sought a more moderate approach to the question of idolatry. The issue had come up in Corinth decades before, as reflected in 1 Corinthians 8 and 10. Perhaps the Nicolaitans, too, argued that since "an idol is nothing" and "there is no God but one" (1 Cor. 8:4 NASB), ingesting meat that had been offered to an idol could not bring genuine spiritual harm to the disciple. They might have remembered the saying of Jesus that "there is nothing outside a person that by going in can defile" (Mark 7:15). Why, then, should Christians—to their own hurt and impoverishment—provoke their neighbors unnecessarily by remaining absent from civic festivals and from dinners in the halls of their associations or the dining rooms where their patrons and friends would hold symposia? While the Christians would still know that "an idol is nothing," their neighbors would no longer think of them as atheists or as antisocial and therefore potentially subversive.

For John, however, the pressing question was not "How far can we go to foster good relations with our non-Christian neighbors and to provide for our own social and economic security?" For him, the question was "How clear can we be in our witness that the worship of any God but the One is absolutely wrong?" Where the Nicolaitans' compromise was adopted, Christians would no longer by their blatant practice confront their neighbors with claims about the reality of the one and only God and the exclusive honors due that God. They would no longer witness against the empty pretensions of Roman imperial ideology, especially as enshrined in the cult of Roma, Augustus, and Augustus's successors. And, we recall, John was also more allergic than his rival prophets to participating at all in an economic system that required the acknowledgment of other gods—and this on top of its already self-serving and exploitative practices.

John accuses these rival teachers of misleading Christ-followers to "practice fornication" (Rev. 2:14, 20 NRSV). While some take this literally, I have doubts that John meant that they were encouraging actual sexual immorality. Yes, parties in the Greco-Roman world could get out of hand. But John has introduced this language as part of his strategy of drawing on the story of Balaam, found in the book of Numbers. Balaam is remembered most famously for having been summoned by Balak, king of Moab, to curse the Hebrews on behalf of the Moabites and Midianites as they arrived from their long desert sojourn and began their invasion of Canaan. But Balaam appears to have been a genuine prophet who could only speak the words God gave him, with the result that he pronounced a divine blessing over the Hebrews three times rather than cursing them (Num. 22–24). While he failed to earn the wages Balak had promised him on this occasion, he appears to have found a different path to success. Balaam is credited with having masterminded the Midianites' plan to lead the people of Israel into worshiping their gods and assimilating with their people, a plan that involved Midianite women seducing Israelite men (Num. 25:1–2; 31:16). John wants his audience to look at the Christian party referred to as the "Nicolaitans" as another Balaam in their midst, leading them to assimilate and, in the process, break faith with the one God (with even more disastrous consequences).

Moreover, John will talk about sexual intercourse and about partnerships, whether with a promiscuous prostitute or as a virgin bride, throughout Revelation in ways that clearly have a figurative meaning. Sexual immorality functions throughout John's work as a metaphor for all improper intercourse with Roman society and its gods. Sexual purity or fidelity represents loyalty to the one God and God's Messiah. In a visionary world in which Roman imperial power and economy are portrayed as a great prostitute (in Greek, *pornē*), the metaphorical implications of leading "my servants to practice fornication" (2:20 NRSV; in Greek, *porneia*) are easy to catch: The Nicolaitans and, in the neighboring city, Jezebel are teaching that one can make some room for idolatry in order to "get into bed" with the brokers of power and wealth around them.

John reminds the Pergamene Christians exactly what power stands ultimately behind all idolatrous ritual: Satan and his demons. The people around them may not "give up worshiping demons and idols of gold and silver and bronze and stone and wood" (9:20), but do the Christians themselves really want to be associated with those practices in light of the day of Christ's appearing? And, John asserts, the Pergamenes live in the city where Satan has his very throne, mentioned twice in this oracle for emphasis (2:13).

A number of notable scholars have read this as a reference to Pergamum's Temple of Roma and Augustus, but this is unlikely. While the imperial cult, and by extension its temples, is of tremendous significance for John and figures prominently throughout Revelation, John has already found a suitable image for this phenomenon—it is the cult of the beast, whom Satan has summoned from the sea, and of the beast's image. Those who identify "the throne of Satan" with the city's most distinctive landmark—the great Altar of Zeus, dominating the city from its position on the acropolis (and, indeed, having the appearance of a great marble throne)—seem to me to be on firmer ground. And, as we have already seen, the identification of the Greek and Roman gods with demons (Ps. 106:37; Bar. 4:6–7; 1 Cor. 10:19–21; Rev. 9:20) would have made it very natural for John to associate the chief of these gods (Zeus/Jupiter) with Satan, the chief of demons. The identification of Satan as the spiritual force behind the imperial power (the many-headed sea-beast) throughout the visions strongly suggests that the "throne of Satan" would reflect some landmark or practice associated more closely with the traditional gods, especially the chief god, Zeus.

John's visions will make the Pergamenes look at many of their local landmarks differently. Their fellow citizens flocked to the sacrifices at the Temples of Athena, Demeter, and Dionysus, but John invites the Christians to see this as the worship of Satan's underlings by deceived and deviant souls (9:20–21). Their fellow citizens took special pride in the activities of the

Temple of Roma and Augustus that had brought them regional recognition as a *neōkoros* city, a pride that would escalate in the coming decades with the construction of the new Temple of Trajan, but this was all a manifestation of the deception of Satan and his local agent on the land (13:11–18). How, then, could the Nicolaitans actually be helping by making room for Christians to edge back toward those settings when they should be fleeing them entirely and warning their neighbors to do likewise?

Formerly, the Pergamene Christians, like those in the other cities, would have been continually overwhelmed by the sight of the majority who did not hold to their commitments, who tried to impress upon the Christians that they were the deviant ones who needed to get in line. After seeing the whole picture again, radiating out from the throne of the one God, the tables are turned. The visions of angels and archangels, of all the company of heaven, and of all creation lauding God and the Lamb (4:1–5, 11; 5:9–14) assure the Christians that they are not the deviant ones, not even the minority report. Formerly, these believers might have allowed themselves to drink in something of the party line about the golden age that Rome restored. Now they are made freshly aware of the undertones to the "official" ideology of the Roman Peace and reminded that they still live in the age dominated by evil powers, awaiting the true and eternal golden age when "the kingdom of the world" becomes "the kingdom of our Lord and of his Messiah" (11:15).

John also paints the prophetess whom he calls "Jezebel" in Babylon's scarlet hues, particularly in regard to "sexual immorality." Jezebel teaches other Christians to "fornicate" (2:20 AT) and has not herself repented "of her fornication" (2:21 AT); Babylon disseminates her defilement through "the wine of the passion of her fornication" (14:8 AT). These verbal associations reinforce John's warning that Jezebel's ministry leads believers into the webs of impure entanglements spun by Rome, with the result that, for the sake of the temporal benefits partnership brings, they will incur a share of responsibility for the injustices of Roman imperialism (18:4). Particularly after experiencing John's visions, getting in bed with Rome would not look nearly so attractive.

As the Pergamene and Thyatiran Christians read their situation in light of Revelation, they were likely to conclude with John that survival was not a matter of developing a theology that allowed for them to eat food sacrificed to idols and to form entangling alliances with the Roman order. It was, rather, a matter of bearing bold and uncompromising witness to the one true God in the midst of the worship of many false gods, of putting one's hope in the coming kingdom of God's Messiah rather than the *Pax Romana*, and of coming out from, and keeping oneself unstained by, Babylon's worldwide web of exploitation.

Laodicea

> Write this to the angel of the church in Laodicea:
>
> "These are the words of the Amen, the faithful and true witness, the ruler [or "beginning"] of God's creation. I know your works. You are neither cold nor hot. I wish that you were either cold or hot. So because you are lukewarm, and neither hot nor cold, I'm about to spit you out of my mouth. After all, you say, 'I'm rich, and I've grown wealthy, and I don't need a thing.' You don't realize that you are miserable, pathetic, poor, blind, and naked. My advice is that you buy gold from me that has been purified by fire so that you may be rich, and white clothing to wear so that your nakedness won't be shamefully exposed, and ointment to put on your eyes so that you may see. I correct and discipline those whom I love. So be earnest and change your hearts and lives. Look! I'm standing at the door and knocking. If any hear my voice and open the door, I will come in to be with them, and will have dinner with them, and they will have dinner with me. As for those who emerge victorious, I will allow them to sit with me on my throne, just as I emerged victorious and sat down with my Father on his throne. If you can hear, listen to what the Spirit is saying to the churches." (3:14–22 CEB)

The imagery of the different temperatures commands a great deal of attention in modern interpretation. One line of interpretation asserts that "hot" represents fervency and zeal in regard to the faith while "cold" represents complete indifference to Christ. Such interpretations are entirely speculative—not to mention implausible, for Christ would not equally commend fervent faithfulness and complete indifference. The oracle, however, does not call for the interpretation of what "hot" and "cold" would precisely represent, only for an understanding of the rhetorical impact of being found so distasteful by Jesus as to be spewed out of his mouth in disgust.

The audience had plenty of experience with waters of different temperatures. Laodicea, like many cities that relied on aqueducts to carry water to its residents from a distance, would have had a typically tepid water supply in contrast to neighboring Colossae's cold water spring or Hierapolis's therapeutic hot springs. It is worth noting, however, that Strabo, an experienced traveler from around the turn of the era, found Laodicea's water to be quite drinkable, whereas he found the water from those local hot springs entirely unsuitable for drinking (*Geography* 13.3.14). Moreover, both hot and cold water would be served at banquets, with tepid water being offered as an emetic between courses (hence a possible connection between the church's lukewarmness and Christ's vomiting them out of his mouth). Those who understand both "hot" and "cold" to represent desirable (if unspecified) qualities, rather than fervor on the one hand and complete indifference on the other, are on firmer ground. This would better reflect the uses of cold and hot water in the first-century social context in general and the local setting of Laodicea in particular: Hierapolis's hot water is considered even today to be healing and salutary; the cold water from Colossae's springs is also welcoming and refreshing.

Though a moral or allegorical approach to the various temperatures has fueled many sermons on this oracle (and will no doubt continue to do so), it seems unlikely that the glorified Christ intended for the temperature reading to be a meaningful part of the diagnosis. Rather, the imagery would have served to shock the Laodicean believers into realizing the magnitude of the spiritual danger that accompanied their condition in the eyes of their Lord. That spiritual danger is then spelled out quite clearly in the verses that follow—and, contrary to their current assessment of themselves, they make Christ sick to his stomach and ready to purge himself of them: "You say, 'I'm rich, and I've grown wealthy, and I don't need a thing.' You don't realize that you are miserable, pathetic, poor, blind, and naked" (3:17 CEB).

The Laodicean Christians are depicted as thinking no differently from other citizens of Laodicea profiting from the economic boom of trade in the imperial period. The proud but deceived person who says "I am rich and need nothing" is known also from Greco-Roman philosophical texts and from the Hebrew prophets. But the Laodiceans' mistaken self-assessment is further reflected in "Babylon's" own self-deception:

> In her heart she says, "I sit like a queen! I'm not a widow. I'll never see grief." This is why her plagues will come in a single day—deadly disease, grief, and hunger. She will be consumed by fire because the Lord God who judges her is powerful. (18:7–8 CEB)

The wealth and plenty of the Roman economy was deceptive: It gave Rome false confidence in its security, a false confidence easily passed along to its partners, among whom the prospering Laodicean Christians would perilously find themselves. They would hear another striking resonance of the glorified Christ's oracle to them near the climax of the pouring out of the seven libation bowls that complete the manifestation of God's just wrath against the ungodliness below: "Look! I'm coming like a thief! Favored are those who stay awake and clothed so that they don't go around naked and exposed to shame" (16:15 CEB; see also 3:18). Like Babylon herself, they were in danger of having their true nakedness—their true poverty and false pride—exposed to their shame, even to their ultimate loss. With Christ's summons to them to buy clothing from him to cover their shame, John disposed them to listen carefully when he spoke of robes being given out, and to discern what changes in practice would be necessary to be found clothed in the white robes of Christ's loyal and courageous witnesses when Christ comes (7:9, 13; 22:14), so as to stand before him with confidence rather than cry out to the hills to cover them and hide them from the searching eyes of God and the Lamb.

Extended Note: The Seven Oracles as Epochs of Church History

It is common for proponents of both the historicist and futurist approaches (discussed in ch. 1) to interpret the seven oracles as seven sequential epochs of church history. This has the advantage of allowing the interpreter to account for the distance between John's setting and the alleged fulfillment of the events recounted in the visions beginning in chapter 4, which is especially important in futurist interpretations. Such readings, however, exhibit a starkly Eurocentric and, more particularly, Protestant-centered perspective. The focus of attention moves from the apostolic age (Ephesus), through the period of persecutions from Nero through Diocletian and Maximian (Smyrna), and through the period of legalization under Constantine (Pergamum). At this point the Western church moves onto center stage to the exclusion of Christianity elsewhere. The oracle to Thyatira characterizes (caricatures) the period of the papacy; the oracle to Sardis speaks of the Western post-Enlightenment church; the oracle to Philadelphia; the Great Awakening and missionary endeavors of England and the United States; and, finally, Laodicea, the lukewarm state of the modern church (again, in the West).

Aside from the gross oversimplification this imposes even upon the Western church, the scheme completely neglects the state of the church in the Southern Hemisphere and the Middle and Far East. The scheme presumes that God, in revealing this information, is really only concerned with the Western church up through the Reformation and thereafter with the Protestant churches, largely in Great Britain and America. If the oracle to Laodicea is meant to characterize the church of the present day, the glorified Christ would be giving no notice to the millions of faithful Christians in the developing world whose fidelity to God under great pressure, and whose enthusiasm for evangelism, far more closely resemble the conditions in Smyrna and Philadelphia than Laodicea.

Regarding each church as representative of the whole church in a particular era grossly caricatures the periods of church history so described. Moreover, there has never been an era in which the diversity of the churches addressed by Revelation—and greater diversity besides—failed to be represented. I find it more prudent to regard the seven churches together as typical of the kinds of congregations one might find throughout the world in any and every age, rather than each one as typical of the entire church in any one period.

Listening for What the Spirit Is Saying to the Churches

The pattern observed in these oracles offers itself as a guide for meditation and study not only focused on the oracles themselves, or only on Revelation as a whole, but on the whole counsel of Scripture as we seek illumination *of* our situation from *outside* our situation:

1. What do we most need to bear in mind about Jesus in order to respond to him and to our particular situation in a manner that is faithfully obedient and fully invested?
2. What are we currently doing that bears effective witness (in our speech, in our deeds, in our relationships) to the Creator God and to Jesus the Redeemer, such that we hear Christ's word of commendation?
3. What are we currently doing, or failing to do, such that this witness is stifled, muted, or betrayed?
4. Where is our loyalty, our zeal, our full-blooded response to Jesus found wanting?

5. What promises from God do we need to keep before our eyes in order to change for the better and respond as would please Christ more fully as he stands in our midst?

John placed the answers to such questions for his own congregations within a thoroughgoing interpretation of their world in the light of God's purposes and just requirements of his creation. John would likely call us to do the same—to seek the same "apocalyptic adjustment" to our view of the world that he sought for himself and passed along to his congregations. Revelation still interprets—and calls us to interpret—the social, political, religious, and economic realities of our everyday experience. It does so not by asking us to equate its images with those realities, playing the endless game of "pin the tail on the antichrist" or trying to line up the seven seals with the broadcasts on CNN or rezoning such-and-such a nation as the real "Babylon." Rather, Revelation invites Christ-followers into the same processes that guided John as he came upon his own "apocalyptic adjustment" to the way he looked at and evaluated the world around him and was thus enabled to communicate this to his congregations, calling them to ever greater levels of covenant faithfulness toward God and the Lamb.

The product of John's engagements—Revelation itself—suggests that his process would commend, at least, the following steps to those who would continue to wrestle alongside him to see their world beyond the blinders of their social location, so as to speak prophetically within and from that location.

Immerse Yourselves in Scripture

John lived in the Hebrew Scriptures. John saw his world in the light of those Scriptures, under which the powers of the world and the practices of the church were all measured in the balance, found wanting, and challenged to close the distance (or, at the very least, indicted for the distance). John was a true steward of the tradition. He was not progressive. He was not practical. He was not adaptive. He did not cater to contemporary trends. There was no room for compromise. But it was John's commitment as a bondservant to the tradition of Israel and of Jesus that had enabled him to break free from the power of the lies of the domination systems into which he and his hearers had been born and bred, and to break their hold over himself and his congregations. These traditions opened his eyes to Roman imperialism in a way that was not possible for a Jezebel or a member of the Nicolaitan circle or most of the Christians in Laodicea, and they gave him a language by means of which to invite others into that liberation from the matrix of Roman imperial propaganda.

Immersing ourselves in the world of Scripture, we run the same risk and we reach for the same prize. We run the risk of being rebuffed as outdated fossils or relics. But we also are given a space in which we can live outside of the values, priorities, and stories of the dominant culture that surrounds us, with its idolization of power, wealth, and self-gratification, and outside of our own stories with the longings, struggles, and distractions they impose upon us. We are given a place where all of these things loosen their hold on us, and from which we can look back at all these things from a different perspective, one that puts them in perspective and empowers us to encounter them as people who will "keep the commandments of God and hold fast to the faith of Jesus" (Rev. 14:12).

Immerse Yourselves in Prayer and Meditation

The encounter with the tradition of the prophets and apostles is vital, but equally vital is the encounter with the living God, which brings that tradition to life and causes it to speak a living word to us, about us, and through us. Listening is the key posture here, as is holding all our convictions about our situation and the many contested issues in our society loosely before God, to allow the Spirit to sift and sort out a genuinely true perspective from the noise that has become so great around us and has invaded our own minds to such an extent.

Revelation also frankly challenges us to entertain a greater openness toward entering into alternate states of consciousness, where God's Spirit can speak to our spirits and consciousness more directly, piecing together what we have gathered from the sacred texts and seen in our lives and the world around us. If we frequent the world of the Scriptures and the heritage of the Christian tradition fully and often, we will be able to exercise appropriate discernment, testing everything and holding on to what is good.

Center Yourselves on God and the Lamb

The path into God's presence remains the discipline of worship and adoration, in the company of the hosts of heaven and of the faithful on earth.

John invited his hearers to enter into multiple scenes of worship so as to find themselves centered on God and the Lamb and, in this manner, to find their way through the challenges of life in Roman Asia without compromising their God-centered orbit. Entering into worship—and letting worship change you, your sense of reality, and your whole orientation to everyday life—is an essential facet of the apocalyptic adjustment that Revelation nurtures.

It is important to qualify this, however, by saying that a "worship service" is not the same as "worship." A worship service fits into the realities of Monday through Saturday (and may even be dull by comparison), but worship puts one in touch with the realities that change Monday through Saturday. Entering into this kind of genuine worship is not as simple as choosing one music style over another or seeking one emotional effect rather than another. Indeed, where the conversation centers on these externals, people seeking life-changing worship are barking up the wrong tree entirely. Rather, it involves becoming so fully aware of God's presence, character, and power that worship is the natural response in ourselves and those around us.

Examine Public Discourse

John knew the power that stories have over the lives of individuals. We seek contexts for our lives, broader contexts that will give them meaning. Domination systems are happy to supply those stories and those hopes that will give us meaning and context, though in such a way as to secure our allegiance—even our servitude—to those systems at the same time. The depth of human allegiance to these national narratives has been on recent display in the American context in the controversies surrounding the preservation of the "old" story that glorifies America's origins and practices as formulated by representatives of the empowered groups over against making room for how the story has been experienced by its marginalized—and, in many instances, victimized—groups.

Revelation suggests three other important contexts—the context of the sacred tradition, the context of gathered worship, and the context of prayer and meditation in the presence of God—in which to locate ourselves and from which to examine the "stories" that representatives of domination systems tell and have told for decades or centuries, the stories into which we have been born. What is the impact upon us, or what are the feelings and inclinations evoked by, the story of America's rise and exercise of sovereignty? How is this story evoked in the context of our political and economic initiatives here and throughout the world? As we immerse ourselves in God's story and God's conversation more fully, in what ways do we begin to hear our own nation's story differently, or see its policies and strategies differently? Revelation demands of us that we raise such questions in regard to our own national ideologies, whatever countries we hail from.

Exercise Vigilance

John watched and critiqued Roman imperialism globally and in its local manifestations in Asia Minor, but he also kept a critical ear and eye open toward the Christian communities. The contexts of Scripture, prayer, and worship—in concert with our prophetic critique of the "spirit of the age" nurtured by the powers around us—position us to exercise more effective vigilance within our own congregations. Part of the ongoing charge of disciples entrusted with any kind of leadership in the church is to keep listening for the Spirit's word concerning things being done well, things being overlooked, things taking a turn away from radical faithfulness, and things providing forthcoming opportunities to bear living testimony to God's love, mercy, and righteousness—all while striving to discern these things in light of the "bigger picture" of who God is, what God wants, and the direction in which God is driving human history.

Reflection

The section "Listening for What the Spirit Is Saying to the Churches" begins with a series of questions based on the pattern found in the seven oracles.

1. Use these questions as an agenda for prayerful discernment and discussion in the setting of a group in your church (a staff meeting, a Bible study group, an administrative committee, etc.).
2. Use these questions as an agenda for reflection on a particular biblical passage outside of Revelation (for example, a passage from the prophets, the teachings of Jesus, or an epistle). These questions may be used both for self-examination and for prayerful reflection on your faith community in light of that passage.

7

John's Proclamation of the One Who Is, Was, and Is Coming: The God of Revelation

John writes to these seven congregations mindful of the well-established practice of testing prophetic utterances. He has himself commended the Ephesian Christians for their examination and rejection of "those who say they are apostles but are not, and you have found them to be liars" (Rev. 2:2 CEB). One important test for evaluating a new revelation was discerning whether or not it aligned with hitherto accepted revelation, whether the apostolic tradition (as in Gal. 1:6–9; 1 John 1:1–4; 4:1–3) or the Scriptures that the apostles themselves accepted (that is, the Jewish Scriptures) and in which they grounded their *own* message. It is to this larger tradition that John and other prophets remain accountable, by which their words are to be tested and either approved or rejected. It is on the basis of their lack of consonance with the larger tradition, and not on the basis of John's alleged authoritarianism, that the guidance of "Jezebel" and the Nicolaitans would be rejected.

John's own prophetic word was not accepted merely because he claims to have "seen" and "heard" what he communicates, though he had probably by this point in his relationship with these seven congregations established his voice as a reliable one. Rather, his prophetic work would have been heeded because what he communicated cohered with the traditions of the Jewish Scriptures and the teachings of Jesus shared by John and his congregations. And the judgment on John must be that his own revelation of God's character, actions, and purposes is overwhelmingly consonant with what he learned from his exposure to the breadth of the Jewish Scriptures. John gives fresh expression to the essential proclamation about God found in the Old Testament, reminding his congregations of God's character, God's just requirements of his creatures, God's patterns of intervention in human affairs, and God's purposes for creation. This becomes the framework within which he assesses—and calls his congregations to assess—the dynamics of the world around them and the most faithful response within their situation.

In this chapter, we will explore Revelation as a brilliant, creative work of theology—a proclamation about the one God known throughout the many streams of Old Testament tradition and the sayings of Jesus, brought together here into one kaleidoscopic presentation by John, whose work as preacher and prophet grows out of his rich understanding of the God of the Scriptures and the God of Jesus. John is not primarily a wild-eyed prophet: He is a theologian. He is a person who knows God—the full picture of the God of Israel and the God of Jesus—better than most people in the seven churches, and perhaps better than most people in any church.

The God Who Is Alone Worthy of Worship

John forcefully proclaims the one God who is alone worthy of worship and targets idolatry as a behavior supremely to be avoided. John speaks in unison with the Shema, the fundamental "creed" of Judaism recited twice daily by pious Jews throughout the ancient world: "Hear, O Israel: The Lord is our God, the LORD alone" (Deut. 6:4). And the Shema is, indeed, a faith claim about the uniqueness of the God of Abraham, Isaac, and Jacob, and the unique right this God has to the loyal obedience of the people: "You shall love the LORD your God with all your heart and with all your soul and with all your might. Keep these words that I am commanding you today" (Deut. 6:5–6).

Foremost among those words are the opening commandments of the Decalogue, the Ten Commandments: "I am the LORD your God. . . . You shall have no other gods before me. You shall not make for yourself an idol, whether in the form of anything that is in heaven above or that is on the earth beneath or that is in the water under the earth. You shall not bow down to them or worship them" (Deut. 5:6–9). The Hebrew Bible is full of commentary upon, and application of, this central summons. It is a theme that pervades historical books (e.g., 2 Kgs. 17:9–18), wisdom literature and liturgical texts (e.g., Pss. 96:1–9; 97:6–7; 115:3–11; 135:13–21; Wis. 13:1–15:17), and the prophetic writings (e.g., Isa. 44:6–24; Jer. 10:1–11). John's heart beats with this same pulse as he manifests his intense concern with keeping "the commandments of God" (Rev. 12:17; 14:12). The first and second of those commandments are foremost in his mind as he calls the churches away from "food sacrificed to idols" (2:14, 20) and from any compromise with idolatry (9:20–21), especially the imperial cult (13:1–18). John gives voice to the eternal call to "fear God and give him glory," to offer God worship as "him who made heaven and earth, and sea and the springs of water" (14:6–7), rather than to offer worship to "the gods who did not make the heavens and the earth" (Jer. 10:11; see also Ps. 96:5).

John's proclamation calls his hearers to examine their own practices of "worship" closely. What do we worship besides God? What claims our allegiance ahead of God? What other things do we value enough that we hold ourselves back in our response to God's call or Jesus's instructions? John particularly focuses on the danger, the lure, of idolatry. This was an ever-present reality in his setting, as it continues to be for the Christian minorities living, for example, in India or Sri Lanka. These believers are surrounded by sacred sites, ancient and modern, built around iconic representations of the divine (that is to say, idols), whether of the Buddha or the gods of the Hindu pantheon. Christians in North America are not confronted with idolatry in its historic form, though there is much to be gained from examining the extent to which we are entangled in more sublimated forms of idolatry. Jesus hinted at this possibility even within the context of monotheistic, anti-iconic Judea and Galilee: "You cannot serve God and Mammon" (Matt. 6:24 RSV)—that is, wealth.

As we consider the breadth of John's own understanding of the God of Israel and the God of Jesus, perhaps it is good also to examine whether we are ourselves worshiping God or, to some extent, more of an image of God. While we are likely not in danger of making a carved image of God for use in worship, we may nevertheless have fallen prey to shaping a *mental* image of God and worshiping this god. The theologians of ancient Israel must have had significant insight into the problem of fashioning any image of the divine to have so forcefully opposed the near-universal tendency to create sculpted images as a means of interacting with the divine and to have sought to eliminate this so completely from the nation's practice. Perhaps that insight included the realizations (1) that no image captures the whole of the thing represented (in this case, the whole of God) and (2) that the partial image inevitably replaces the real whole. Encounter with the divine is thereby not facilitated in the end but distorted and interrupted.

John's proclamation of God's character, interests, and interventions, rooted in so many streams of the scriptural tradition, may challenge us in regard to our images of God. Is our image of God as multifaceted, as complete, as John's? Or do we carry about and worship a personal image of God, a favorite mental picture of God, that has replaced the larger reality of who God is? Some may worship only the God of love and acceptance who makes no demands in terms of our own commitment to justice and holiness. Some may worship a God of personal salvation who seeks individual decisions, but who is not concerned about fair access for all to what is necessary for a life with dignity. Still others may worship the God who is available to them when they want assurance that they're not alone or when they want help or comfort in life's difficulties, but not the God to whom they must keep themselves available to serve (and not simply *be* served by). One of John's often overlooked contributions to Christian theology and the Christian practice that is shaped by theology is his weaving together of so many different facets of God, inviting us thereby to draw closer to the full reality.

The God Who Indicts Domination Systems

The label "domination system" has come to be applied to systemic social arrangements that institutionalize unequal power relationships and that use those power relationships in the interest of the empowered, often to the detriment of the less empowered or unempowered. Domination systems are the standard operating modes of societies that have ordered themselves around the goals of securing the privilege of the few, or the pursuit of wealth or power by the few, as the highest considerations. Such orderings of a society lead inevitably to disregard for the fair distribution of this world's goods and disregard for the socially, politically, and economically vulnerable. These systems develop their own "logic" into which they typically indoctrinate all participants, so that ongoing commitment to the system is assured even by those who are most disadvantaged by the system. They are often accompanied by ideologies of self-aggrandizement, if not self-worship, that also serve to mask the costs of the systems in terms of human suffering and dignity.

Examples of domination systems include militarism, the willingness to kill (or that another person be killed) in order that my own interests should be protected; capitalism (alongside other economic "isms"), the willingness for others to lose access even to a secure and stable livelihood in order that my own enjoyment of excess be protected; and environmental consumption, the willingness for future generations (and many present populations) to find themselves in an ecologically less secure position so that I can keep enjoying the profits and conveniences that I enjoy.[1]

John's indictment of Rome (Rev. 17–18) is entirely in keeping with the Hebrew prophetic tradition in which God sets himself against any society that promotes an elite's pursuit of wealth or power as the highest consideration. This strain emerges throughout the Major Prophets, particularly in those texts upon which John draws (e.g., Isa. 23; 47; Jer. 51; Ezek. 26–27). It is rooted in the exodus event itself, when God took the side of an oppressed and enslaved people, at the cost of whose dehumanization the great treasure cities of Egypt were being constructed (the treasures of Egypt themselves often coming from violent conquest, enforced tribute, and oppressive practices of internal taxation and conscripted labor). The classical prophets not only turned this critical eye to foreign powers but also indicted Israel when it put the enjoyment of luxury by the few ahead of the survival of the many, or when it forgot the covenant loyalty due God, reveling instead in its alliances with international powers that allowed the elites to achieve greater economic growth or political influence.

From his close reading of these prophets, John has discerned what the response of the God of the prophets would be to a new, grander, more overtly self-deifying, and more violently expansive domination system—namely, the Roman Empire. He brings those prophetic traditions to bear on the situation facing his congregations to help them see their context in light of those paradigms of violent oppression, luxurious overconsumption, and self-legitimating ideology (Rev. 17:1–18:24).

John was not alone in presenting such a close correspondence between Roman domination and the prophetic critique of empire. The authors of 4 Ezra and 2 Baruch came to the same conclusion regarding Rome's status in the sight of the one God on the basis of their reading of the Hebrew scriptural tradition as well. The author of 4 Ezra also talks about Rome in connection with the four beasts of Daniel 7 (4 Ezra 12:11–12), though somewhat differently from John, as he makes Rome the fourth beast rather than a combination of all four. Nevertheless, he writes:

> You, the fourth [beast] that has come, have conquered all the beasts that have gone before, and you have held sway over the world with great terror, and over

1. Helpful introductions to domination systems, their rules of operation, and their effects include: C. Dale White, *Making a Just Peace: Human Rights & Domination Systems* (Abingdon, 1988); Walter Wink, *Naming the Powers* (Fortress, 1983); Walter Wink, *Unmasking the Powers* (Fortress, 1986); Walter Wink, *Engaging the Powers* (Augsburg Fortress, 1992); and Wes Howard-Brook and Anthony Gwyther, *Unveiling Empire: Reading Revelation Then and Now* (Orbis, 1999).

> all the earth with grievous oppression, and for so long you have lived on the earth with deceit. You have judged the earth but not with truth, for you have oppressed the meek and injured the peaceable; you have hated those who tell the truth and have loved liars; you have destroyed the homes of those who brought forth fruit and have laid low the walls of those who did you no harm. Your insolence has come up before the Most High and your pride to the Mighty One. . . . Therefore you, eagle, will surely disappear . . . so that the whole earth, freed from your violence, may be refreshed and relieved. (2 Esdras 11:40–46)[2]

The charges of violence, oppression, deception, and pride are essentially the same (John will dwell more upon luxurious consumption, in addition) and suggest that deep immersion in the Hebrew scriptural tradition led two apocalypticists independently to one inescapable conclusion concerning the domination system of Roman imperialism.

John's proclamation of a God who opposes domination systems challenges hearers in every age to examine themselves and their practices lest they be found among those who profit from and are privileged by such systems, and who will therefore receive their share in God's judgment of the same (Rev. 18:4). Do we maintain a sufficient distance from the political, economic, and ideological systems that seek our allegiance and participation such that we can recognize the ways in which they inflict harm on others? Do we take up our stand alongside God, God's prophets like John, and Jesus himself against the practices that safeguard the interests of some at the expense of others and that thereby interfere with God's good vision for all people?

The God of the Exodus

The importance of the exodus story for shaping the Jewish people's knowledge of God cannot be overestimated. Its centrality is evident from the opening words of the Decalogue: "I am the Lord your God, who brought you out of the land of Egypt, out of the house of slavery; you shall have no other gods before me" (Exod. 20:2–3; see also Deut. 5:6–7). The exodus story, as a revelation of the character of God and God's interventions, was held continually before the

2. The book presented in the NRSVue, CEB, and other modern translations as "2 Esdras" is actually a composite work. The middle portion (2 Esdras 3–14) is a Jewish apocalypse from about 100 CE and is independently known as "4 Ezra." This is the work in focus here. Two Christian additions round out "2 Esdras" as found in the NRSVue: a second-century Christian apocalypse (2 Esdras 1–2 = 5 Ezra), and a third-century Christian appendix (2 Esdras 15–16 = 6 Ezra).

worshiping community in its Psalms (see, e.g., Pss. 78, 105, 106) and canticles (e.g., the Song of Moses in Exod. 15:1–18). Prophets regularly invoked the exodus as the beneficent act in which the obligations of the covenant were grounded (e.g., Ezek. 20:3–26) and as the precedent for the hope of a new exodus from the Babylonian captivity (as in Isa. 40:3–5; 43:16–19; 52:1–6).

John stands in line with this tradition, proclaiming the One seated upon the throne as the God of the exodus, who now works the final deliverance of God's people in a definitive exodus. John draws his description of the Christian communities as "a kingdom and priests serving our God" (Rev. 5:10; see also 1:5–6) from God's address to the exodus generation, calling them to be "for me a priestly kingdom" (Exod. 19:6). John shares in the Christian conviction that this priestly kingdom transcends ethnic identity, being constituted not merely by Jacob's descendants, but by people drawn from "every tribe and language and people and nation" (Rev. 5:9). The plagues that God visits upon the inhabitants of the earth in the seven trumpets and seven bowls recall, in many of their particulars, the plagues visited upon Egypt in Exodus 7:14–10:29. These include the return of plagues involving boils (Exod. 9:10; Rev. 16:2), water turning to blood (Exod. 7:20–21; Rev. 16:3–4), darkness (Exod. 10:21; Rev. 16:10), frogs (Exod. 8:2–3; Rev. 16:13), and hailstones (Exod. 9:24; Rev. 16:21). As in Exodus, the plagues are meant to induce repentance, though they are once again unsuccessful in this regard (Exod. 8:15, 19, 32, etc.; Rev. 9:20–21; 16:9, 11, 21).

By drawing these correspondences, John may be seeking not so much to communicate about the specific ways in which God will punish a rebellious world, but rather to shape the hearers' understanding of the character of the world in which they are living. What does it say about the condition of the people of God under Roman rule that God should find it necessary to bring all the plagues of Egypt again upon the world? John depicts future consequences in order to communicate something about present causes. Roman Asia Minor, and indeed Roman imperialism as a whole, imposes a state of oppression. The people of God need deliverance from that system; they do not need to seek avenues for cooperation with that system (as, for example, the rival teachers in Pergamum and Thyatira are urging). Indeed, partnership is impossible, for the parties involved are oppressive taskmasters and subjugated peoples who are not even permitted to worship as their God requires. At the same time, John is invoking the historical precedent of the exodus to assure Christ-followers that God is indeed deeply concerned with the plight of God's people and will intervene for their liberation from the domination systems of the world. As in Exodus, the people of God are sealed for protection from the plagues (Rev. 7:1–8; 9:4; 16:2). The marking of the doorposts and lintels of the Hebrews' houses with the blood of the (Passover) lamb is the most striking image associated therewith (Exod. 12:7, 12–13), but God's protection was evident also when the plagues did not affect the land, livestock, and human inhabitants of Goshen, where the Hebrews resided (Exod. 8:22–23; 9:6–7, 25–26; 10:22–23).

Perhaps it is significant that Moses's pretext for the exodus was the need for his people to worship God beyond the borders of Egypt, since the Hebrews and Egyptians cherished mutually offensive religious practices (Exod. 5:3; 7:16; 8:1, 20, 25–27; 9:13; 10:3, 7–11). In Revelation's new exodus, worship remains a primary concern—one that again involves separation from the rites cherished by the oppressor (e.g., 13:11–18; 14:9–11). The redeemed finally sing of God's deliverance by the side of a new sea (15:2–4), with the song of Moses now linked with the song of the Lamb. The exodus, seen also through the tradition of the new exodus of Isaiah in which the faithful are brought out of Babylon (Rev. 18:4–8) and into a new land of promise (Rev. 21:1–22:5), becomes the framework within which to speak of a much grander deliverance.

If John successfully broadens our image of God to make room for the God of the exodus, it follows that our practice of following a God whose character includes such concerns must be broadened correspondingly. And so we might examine ourselves: To what extent are we in touch with the many in this world who desperately need such deliverance from oppression? Have we, like Moses, left Pharaoh's courts and palaces to see the plight of God's people beyond our places of comfort? Have we, like Moses, turned against "our own" in the spaces of privilege because we are so grieved at the plight of the exploited, the oppressed, the people consigned to poverty or starvation, the people thrown in prison because they threaten the privileged? Have we the faith of Moses and of John in the God of the exodus, such that we choose oppression alongside God's people in Goshen, rather than continue to carry on pleasantly in Egypt in ignorance or apathy?

The God Who Vindicates God's Faithful Ones

The psalmists expressed confidence in God's commitment not only to deliver God's people collectively when they fell into distress or oppression, but also to deliver each faithful one from his or her distress: "Many are the afflictions of the righteous person, but the Lord rescues him or her from them all" (Ps. 34:19, AT). The underlying rationale for such bold confidence derives ultimately from Deuteronomy, which promised that covenant loyalty would result in the safe enjoyment of the land and, when that was threatened, God's aid. This promise is echoed throughout the wisdom tradition (e.g., Prov. 3:1–11) and in the Psalms as well.

In seasons of distress, whether from natural calamity or hostile aggression, the faithful would wait expectantly for God's intervention. Their knowledge that they had walked in line with God's commandments (often coupled with the suspicion that their enemies did not) gave them the grounds for expecting deliverance. Since God was just, God would necessarily intervene to bring the promised blessings to the righteous and just punishment to the wicked. If the ungodly gained ascendancy over the righteous person, the cry went up for vindication:

> How long, O LORD? Will you forget me forever? How long will you hide your face from me? How long must I bear pain in my soul and have sorrow in my heart all day long? How long shall my enemy be exalted over me? (Ps. 13:1–2)

The just God could not allow the wicked to put the righteous person to shame and to gain honor or profit at the expense of the godly or the weak (see Pss. 35:24–26; 94:1–6). This same conviction found expression in regard to the fortunes of the nation as well: The cry for vindication can go up on behalf of the slain and the oppressed of the entire nation (as in Ps. 79).

Around 169 to 167 BCE, in the years immediately prior to the outbreak of the Maccabean Revolt, pious Jews were being martyred under the Greco-Syrian king Antiochus IV and his renegade Jewish deputies (see 2 Macc. 6–7), often in a degrading and painful manner. They endured such treatment as a result of their steadfast refusal to break faith with their covenant God. In this context, the expectation arose that the righteous person's commitment to God would be vindicated *after* death, if God's justice had not been manifested in his or her life on *this* side of death. The righteous would be rewarded with the covenant blessings in the life beyond death, and their lawless persecutors would be punished and made to acknowledge the nobility and wisdom of the righteous ones whom they mocked and killed (see 2 Macc. 7:9, 11, 14, 17, 19, 23, 31, 35–36; 4 Macc. 9:8–9, 32; 10:11, 15; 12:11–12; 17:4–6; Wis. 1:16–5:23).

When John depicts the souls of the righteous, slain for the sake of God's word, crying out for vindication (Rev. 6:9–11), he stands in line with this tradition, confessing the justice of God and, therefore, the expectation of God's intervention to uphold the cause of the righteous. He stands firmly in the tradition that claims that even death is insufficient to thwart God's commitment to give justice to those who had walked faithfully in line with God's commandments: "How long, holy and true Sovereign, will you not give judgment and require our blood from the inhabitants of the earth?!" (6:10 AT). As the narrative unfolds, John affirms the truthfulness of the tradition's foundational premises: God is indeed just in all God's ways (15:2–4), as will be seen when God dramatically avenges the blood of God's holy ones. When an angel pours out the third of the seven libation bowls containing the final expression of God's wrath against the injustice of earth's inhabitants, all the waters on earth are turned to blood. The angel exclaims: "You are just, O Holy One, who are and were, for you have judged these things; because they shed the blood of saints and prophets, you have given them blood to drink. It is what they deserve!" (16:5–6). The martyrs themselves, now vindicated, confirm God's justice, adding their "Amen" from beneath the altar to the angel's declaration (16:7). The scenes of God's judgment throughout Revelation are anchored in this traditional expectation that God vindicates God's servants, an expectation relevant to the violence that the Christian communities had endured and would yet endure (2:10, 13; 6:9–11; 11:18; 13:15–17; 17:6; 18:24).

When we read texts that speak about God's vindication of God's own, we may tend to think first about the ways in which we feel we need vindication by God to some degree. But this facet of the God proclaimed by John may also call us to look once again beyond ourselves to sisters and brothers in much greater need of vindication, since they suffer significant loss and disgrace for their commitment to stand alongside Christ in their contexts. In my own context at Ashland Theological Seminary, thanks in large measure to colleagues who have been committed to the global church and to raising awareness about the needs of the same, and in part to personal connections abroad, I hear regularly about the plight of Christians whose contexts are unsupportive of their religious commitments at best, and explicitly intolerant and repressive at worst. If our God is the God who will vindicate them, how should that lead us, as servants of God, to include them in our care? How might we find ways to stand alongside them, encourage them, lobby here to raise awareness of and perhaps even foster intervention in their predicament? How might we show ourselves to be their family, not merely in word but also in deed through our commitment to and investment in them?

The God Who Exercises Sovereign Rule over the Cosmos

John proclaims God as the *Pantokratōr* (Rev. 1:8; 4:8; 11:15; 15:3, etc.), the One who holds all things within his grasp. This God appears consistently as one sitting enthroned (4:2, 9, 10; 5:1, 7, 13; 6:16, etc.), a posture that communicates God's reign over the cosmos. Once again, Revelation is entirely consonant with the witness of the scriptural tradition, particularly highlighted in the Psalms, which keep God's rule in the forefront of the worshipers' consciousness.

> The LORD is king. . . . Your throne is established from of old. (Ps. 93:1–2)
>
> The LORD is king. (Ps. 97:1; 99:1)

God sits in heavenly session, presiding over a court populated by supernatural beings who stand in readiness to do God's bidding and pay God homage as sovereign:

> Bless the LORD, O you his angels, you mighty ones who do his bidding, obedient to his spoken word. Bless the LORD, all his hosts, his ministers that do his will. (Ps. 103:20–21)
>
> Praise him, all his angels; praise him, all his host! (Ps. 148:2)
>
> Blessed are you in the temple of your holy glory, . . . who look into the depths from your throne on the cherubim (Sg. Three 31–32)

Songs such as the last one were inspired by the physical representations of God's enthronement in the first temple, where the space above the ark of the covenant, the top of which was decorated with the two cherubim, represented the throne of the God who "sits enthroned upon the cherubim" (Ps. 99:1; see also Isa. 37:16). Visionaries like Isaiah elaborate upon this, describing visions of God upon this throne, surrounded by multiple angelic beings offering ceaseless worship (Isa. 6:1–6). Ezekiel gives a rather different, more daringly detailed and more colorful depiction of the same (Ezek. 1:4–28). The author of the Testament of Levi, a Jewish text from the first century BCE and one of the Testaments of the Twelve Patriarchs, elaborates still further. There we find a vision of God enthroned in the highest heaven, surrounded by several distinct orders of angels performing different functions within the heavenly court—all visually expressive of God's rule over the cosmos. John's vision of the enthroned One, and of the activity of the orders of heavenly beings around the throne, stands firmly in line with this tradition.

The Hebrew Scriptures consistently affirm that God's sovereign rule brings justice to human affairs. The liturgical traditions of Israel particularly emphasize God's reign expressing itself in judgment, judging the earth, the nations, and their peoples:

> He will judge the peoples with equity. . . . He will judge the world with righteousness and the peoples with his truth. (Ps. 96:10, 13)
>
> Righteousness and justice are the foundation of his throne. (Ps. 97:2)
>
> He is coming to judge the earth. He will judge the world with righteousness and the peoples with equity. (Ps. 98:9)
>
> The Lord is king. . . . He sits enthroned upon the cherubim. . . . Mighty King, lover of justice, you have established equity; you have executed justice. (Ps. 99:1, 4)

John also foregrounds this particular aspect of God's rule. The "good news" about God's accession to the reins of the kingdoms of this world is that God's justice will be manifested in this human sphere:

> We give thanks to you, Lord God Almighty [*Pantokratōr*], the one who is and the "he was," because you have taken up your great power and exercised sovereign rule. And the nations were enraged, and your wrath came, and the right time to judge the dead, and to give the reward to your slaves, to the prophets and the holy ones and those fearing your name, the small and the great, and to ravage the ravagers of the earth. (Rev. 11:16–18 AT)
>
> Alleluia! The deliverance and the glory and the power of our God! Because he judged the great Prostitute, who ravaged the earth in her fornication, and he required the blood of his slaves from her hand. Alleluia! Because the Lord God, the *Pantokratōr*, exercised sovereign rule. (19:1–2, 6 AT)

God's exercise of punitive judgment makes way for a new order of human community, as the latter hymn goes on to celebrate the coming marriage feast of the Lamb (19:7–8), which leads in turn to the vision of the new Jerusalem, a multinational human community "done right."

Worship of the One seated upon the throne is, of course, a spiritual practice that invites us to examine our lives for signs of reflecting the reality of God's rule, or, alternatively, the rule of self-determination and looking out for our own interests rather than God's interests. But since the coming of God's kingdom also means the breaking in of God's justice throughout this world, John would challenge us to examine our alignment here in particular. Are we sufficiently in touch with the injustice faced by our sisters and brothers somewhere in this world to know from the heart what it really means to cry out "Your kingdom come!" to God in prayer on their behalf? In what ways do we put ourselves at God's disposal, for God to use us as agents and instruments for advancing the cause of his kingdom—his justice—in their situation? John's vision—of elites and merchants lamenting but heaven rejoicing at God's judgment of the domination systems of Rome (Rev. 18:9–20; 19:1–3)—radically challenges us to examine our own alignment, whether it is more fully with the perpetrators or with the victims of injustice and oppression in this world.

The God Who Promises Shalom in God's Presence

God's reign moves toward establishing the order in the natural and human spheres that reflects God's just character and God's designs for human community in relationship with the divine. In Revelation, this finds its full expression in the vision of the new Jerusalem, where God's promises to God's people and, indeed, to the nations are finally brought to their full realization.

The image of this consummation as the wedding of God and God's people was poignantly expressed by the prophet Hosea (2:14–20), whose own actions toward his wayward wife, Gomer, became a living parable of God's intentions toward Israel. Isaiah applies this image more particularly to Jerusalem as the bride of God in the context of God's vindication of the fortunes of God's people:

> The Lord delights in you, and your land shall be married. For as a young man marries a young woman, so shall your builder marry you, and as the bridegroom rejoices over the bride, so shall your God rejoice over you. (62:4–5)

The tradition of the covenant as a wedding or marriage comes to expression in early Christian thought as the wedding of Christ to the people of God, with the eschatological age being depicted as a wedding banquet. This has strong roots in the Jesus tradition (Matt. 22:1–14 and parallels) and blends with the tradition of Zion/Jerusalem as God's bride in John's visions of "the holy city, the new Jerusalem, coming down out of heaven from God, prepared as a bride adorned for her husband" (Rev. 21:2; see also 19:6b–9; 21:9; 22:17).

The very idea of the "new heavens and a new earth," together with the passing away of the "former things" and the re-creation of Jerusalem, reprises the hope expressed by Isaiah (65:17–18). When John represents the speech of "a great voice from the throne" announcing this great consummation, he speaks entirely in the language of the prophets who had previously communicated this hope:

> Look—the tent of God is with humankind, and he will make his home with them, and they will be his people, and God himself will be with them, and he will wipe away every tear from their eyes, and death will no longer be, nor grief, nor crying, neither will there be suffering, because the former things passed away. (Rev. 21:3–4 AT)

Several promises previously articulated in God's name would be recognizable: "I will dwell in your midst" (Zech. 2:11); "I will walk among you and will be your God, and you shall be my people" (Lev. 26:11–12 ESV); "Then they shall be my people, and I will be their God" (Ezek. 11:20); "My dwelling place shall be over them, and I will be their God, and they shall be my people" (Ezek. 37:27); "Then the LORD God will wipe away the tears from all faces" (Isa. 25:8); "No more shall the sound of weeping be heard in it [Jerusalem], or the cry of distress" (Isa. 65:19). In the promise to "the one who overcomes" that immediately follows in Revelation 21:7—namely, that "I will be to him or her a God, and he or she will be to me a son or a daughter" (AT)—the hearers encounter the familiar promise from 2 Samuel 7:14 ("I will be a father to him, and he shall be a son to me"), applied first to the Davidic dynasty, then to the Messiah, and here extended to the whole of the Christian community in keeping with the theme of the "people of the holy ones" sharing in the rule of God's Anointed (Dan. 7:27). God's promises will not fail. God will usher in a fully restored community.

John differs from his sources in two significant particulars. The first of these concerns the scope of God's promises, which for John includes men and women from every tribe, language group, people, and nation (5:9–10; 7:9; 14:6–7), rather than reflecting God's particular investment in the one ethnic people of Israel. This is in keeping, of course, with some prophetic voices (like those heard in Isa. 60:3–5 and Zech. 2:11–12) against others (like Ezekiel's in 37:27–28), but stands all the more in line with major streams of early Christian interpretation of the Hebrew scriptural hope (e.g., Luke 3:1–6; Acts 10–11, 15; Rom. 15:7–13; Gal. 3:1–4:7; Eph. 3:1–6; 1 Pet. 2:4–10).

The second point of divergence is more pronounced—namely, the emphatic absence of a temple in the new Jerusalem. This contrasts starkly with Ezekiel, who devotes nine chapters to describing how the perfect temple would be constructed and its rites observed (Ezek. 40–48). This divergence is all the more striking given the other similarities between John's vision and Ezekiel's vision of the new or restored Jerusalem, both involving an angelic being with a measuring rod ushering the seer around the complex and exploring every gate, wall, and structure. John, however, has a clear rationale for this difference (Rev. 21:22): The full presence of God and the Lamb in this city eliminates the need for a temple, since the limits on access to God implied by the temple structure (see Heb. 9:1–8) have been completely transcended in God's perfect future.

These visions communicate something about God's ultimate purposes for human community and thus invite us to examine ourselves in terms of our investment in cooperating with those purposes. How do we make room for God's shalom to break into our world? How do we create room for God to draw near to people from every nation and language group, and for people from every nation and language group to draw near to God and to one another in reconciliation and in mutual investment in the other's wholeness? Where do we work to create spaces and "alternative communities" where Babylon's agenda, values, and power do not dominate—seeking to form at least temporary experiences of community built around Jesus's and the apostles' vision for (and commands to bring about) an alternative way of living together?

The God Whose Patience Has an End

It is not John's visions of cosmic renewal and healing that elicit criticism of his voice, but rather his claims about certain groups of people being cast into the lake of fire or barred from entering the new Jerusalem because they chose a different path than the one he promotes. These were the visions that set D. H. Lawrence on edge, as he condemned John for betraying the New Testament vision of love with his "lake of burning brimstone in which devils, demons, beasts, and bad men should frizzle and suffer for ever and ever and ever, Amen!"[3] These are the claims that continue to evoke accusations of John's bullying audiences into submitting to his authority among modern scholars. The framers of the Revised Common Lectionary could not even permit one verse from Revelation that speaks of exclusion alongside inclusion, omitting

3. Lawrence, *Apocalypse*, 117.

22:15 from the reading of 22:12–21 on the seventh Sunday of Easter—ironically also eliminating the reading of those verses that warn against the strategic omission of problematic verses (22:18–19)!

And yet, even in Revelation's most objectionable parts—those words that rub most gratingly against our cultural values of tolerance and pluralism—even here John does no more than speak in line with the tradition of which he has become the curator and spokesperson. When he proclaims a God who, having created a just kingdom, excludes, punishes, or destroys that which is unjust, rebellious, and not aligned with God, he faithfully portrays that "other side" of God that shows through the Torah, the former and latter prophets, and, ultimately, Jesus himself.

In Isaiah's celebration of the new exodus that God would make for God's people, the prophet includes a note of exclusivity concerning God's new highway through the desert: "The unclean shall not travel on it" (35:8). When the same prophet describes the renewed Jerusalem, he calls Zion to rejoice in part because "the uncircumcised and the unclean shall enter you no more" (52:1). In Ezekiel, immediately following the promise that "they shall be my people, and I will be their God," God turns his attention to those "whose heart goes after their detestable things and their abominations," who will be excluded from the renewed Jerusalem (11:20–21).

In keeping with their awareness that God's city and restored temple precincts are holy, Isaiah and Ezekiel speak of the exclusion of those who are "polluted." John's vision of the "holy city" in which God dwells in all of God's fullness, therefore, quite naturally invites similar discussion of classes of pollution that disqualify one from approaching the Holy One in the holy places of God's dwelling. John's lists (Rev. 21:8, 27; 22:15), however, are notable insofar as they involve not ritual pollution but moral failure, whether the failure to abstain from Babylon's corruption ("murderers and fornicators and sorcerers and idolaters and all liars," 21:8; see also 22:15) or the failure to take a courageous and loyal stand for God and God's Christ ("the cowardly, the faithless," 21:8; "everyone loving and living a lie," 22:15 AT). In this manner, John's lists align with the broadening of the scope of God's salvation to members of any and every nation who keep God's commandments and faith with Jesus (John does not exclude "the uncircumcised" as such, as do Isaiah and Ezekiel).

Above all, John's proclamation of a God who holds rebellious humanity accountable for its affronts against God's honor and rightful claim to obedience resonates with the sayings of Jesus. Matthew 13:41–43 is a case in point:

> The Son of Man will send his angels, and they will gather together out of his kingdom all the stumbling blocks and those practicing unlawfulness and will throw them into the fiery furnace [see Dan. 3:6]: weeping and gnashing of teeth shall be there. Then the righteous will shine like the sun in the kingdom of their Father. Let the one with ears listen. (AT)

Jesus's exclusion of "the stumbling blocks and those practicing unlawfulness" from the kingdom of the Son of Man corresponds quite closely with Revelation 21:8, 27, and 22:15. John simply defines more precisely what constitutes a stumbling block or unlawfulness in his pastoral situation.

Furthermore, Jesus describes the place of exclusion in terms suggesting severe pain and torment: "They will throw them into the furnace of fire, where there will be weeping and gnashing of teeth," a detail not suggestive of quick incineration (Matt. 13:42). Revelation 14:9–11 elaborates this image of judgment by the Messiah, again with specific infractions identified, very much in line with the first commandments of the Decalogue—namely, the prohibitions against worshiping other gods and making cult images for worship.

At the close of Jesus's "Apocalyptic Discourse" in Matthew 24–25, in what is perhaps the most vivid description of the "last judgment" in the New Testament, the Son of Man sends away those who have failed to return gratitude to him in the persons of the hungry, naked, homeless, and imprisoned, to a place of endless torment—the "eternal fire prepared for the devil and his angels" (25:41). This closely resembles the "lake of fire" in Revelation, also populated by both Satan, his minions, and those human beings deceived by him (14:9–11; 19:20; 20:10, 14–15). John is not, in these regards, more exclusive or vindictive than Jesus himself (at least as Jesus is represented in the traditions attributed to him in the Gospels).

The question here is not whether John's vision is profoundly disturbing, but whether John is fairly representing and applying the traditions of the Jewish Scriptures, Jesus, and the early church—or giving expression to violence, hatred, or venom in a manner that betrays the tradition. And, in light of John's alignment with the Hebrew Scriptures, the Jesus tradition, and the apostolic tradition in so many points, it is also hardly the case that John is merely bullying his hearers to get them to accept "his" views. John faithfully portrays a facet of God that many find distasteful—a facet that, though reflected throughout the Scriptures of both Testaments, many exclude from the image of the God they worship. Nevertheless, John's proclamation challenges us to ask: If we are to worship the God known in the whole counsel of Scripture, do we stand in need of recovering a reasonable fear of God, a healthy respect for God's justice and God's power that will keep a fire kindled within us to get in line with God's agenda sooner rather than later, more rather than less, to the degree that God merits rather than to the degree we can comfortably accommodate? John's emphasis on judgment—and that primarily in terms of what we have *done* rather than what we have *believed*—challenges us to examine whether we are really hearing and heeding the words of Jesus when he says, "Why do you call me 'Lord, Lord,' and do not do what I tell you?" (Luke 6:46) or, near Revelation's close, "My reward is with me, to repay according to everyone's work" (22:12).

Reflection

Each of the seven sections in this chapter ends with questions or other prompts calling for examination of how we think about God. Take some time to think through these questions and prompts, particularly with a view to identifying those facets of God that have not been cut deeply into your own God-image, and the implications for your life of serving the God who possesses those qualities, interests, and commitments. Some find it helpful to write down such reflections in a journal for later review, expansion, and accountability. Use these questions also as a basis for discussion in a study group, if you are part of one.

8

Revelation, Politics, and Christian Witness

Our exploration of Revelation as a word to its audiences in first-century Roman Asia clearly demonstrates that the book had immediate and direct political significance for Christ-followers living in that context. William Stringfellow went so far as to claim that "except for the accounts of the Crucifixion of Jesus Christ in the Gospels, Revelation is manifestly the most political part of the New Testament."[1] As John lifted the veil of the propaganda spun both from the imperial center and the circles of the local elites, which was embraced wholeheartedly by the majority of the population around them (and by not a few of the Christ-followers themselves), his book very much became, among other things, a "political" manifesto. The professions of allegiance and the visible actions that would constitute the "witness" that he was anxious for his hearers to preserve would also inevitably have political as well as religious significance.

At the same time, the political meaning and relevance of Revelation is not limited to its first-century context. The political and economic realities it addressed would take shape repeatedly throughout history, however altered in form. We have illuminating examples of modern prophetic voices bringing John's critique of the political machines of his time and John's summons to faithful witness in response to the same to bear on the politics of the post-World War II period. William Stringfellow applied Revelation's word powerfully to the landscape of the United States of the Vietnam era, to the military-economic machine that sustained itself at the cost of countless human lives, and to the "babel" of political propaganda that obscured the truths that would challenge that machine. Allan Boesak brought Revelation's

1. William Stringfellow, *An Ethic for Christians and Other Aliens in a Strange Land* (Word, 1976), 27.

word to bear on the situation of non-white people in apartheid South Africa, where state-sponsored oppression and persecution—legitimated by many white churches—again sustained a grossly unjust system and made its critics disappear. Wes Howard-Brook and Anthony Gwyther engaged John's prophetic word to draw back the veil from the new economic empire captured by the catchphrase "global capital."[2] For all of these writers, it was never a matter of "identifying" facets of their setting with the details in Revelation. John was allowed to speak within and to his first-century audiences. The discovery of analogous actors, dynamics, and situations allowed his word to continue to speak to twentieth- and twenty-first-century audiences.

Admittedly, reading any political-economic system through the lens of Revelation will privilege—and possibly amplify—its darker, demonic aspects. Nevertheless, Revelation, while only one canonical voice, provides an important counter-perspective. While Paul affirms that "there is no authority except from God" (Rom. 13:1), John reminds us that God is not the only invisible power operative upon and through these authorities. There is also the dragon, who summons political-economic-ideological beasts for his own purposes (Rev. 12:17–13:1). The scriptural witness thus reminds us that the actions of political authorities can range from serving God's purposes to open rebellion against God, God's Anointed, and God's people (13:4–8; 17:13–14). It is of great importance, therefore, to allow "God [to use] Revelation to illumine our theological and political landscape"[3] alongside other scriptural witnesses to the authority of the state, and to help us discern the path of faithful engagement with these powers as those whose allegiance is ultimately to Another.

At the same time, we need to take careful stock of the distance between the circumstances under which John's first-century audience lived and those of John's twenty-first-century audiences. In many nations, particularly those where allegiance to Jesus provokes overt hostility and even state-sponsored persecution, that distance is quite narrow, perhaps even imperceptible. The distance is great, however, in Western democracies, where Christians enjoy the same rights and access to political processes as other citizens. Indeed, many of our most eschatologically minded Christian leaders—those most drawn to Revelation themselves, though generally from a very different perspective than the one advocated in this book—are often well-connected

2. Stringfellow, *Ethic*; Allan A. Boesak, *Comfort and Protest: Reflections on the Apocalypse of John of Patmos* (Westminster, 1987); Howard-Brook and Gwyther, *Unveiling Empire*.

3. Kraybill, *Apocalypse*, 22.

within the political, economic, and social networks of the dominant culture, even to the point of frequenting the White House and Capitol Hill. Since Revelation exerts a strong influence on many Christians, some of whom exert, in turn, a strong influence upon American politics, the question is not *whether* to apply Revelation but *how* to apply it in a manner that reflects John's purposes—that is, in a way that *challenges* modern domination systems.

In this chapter, I will revisit some of the more direct ways in which John addressed the political situation of first-century Roman Asia and how he positioned the Christ-followers within his orbit to respond to its challenges. From there, I will offer suggestions concerning how Revelation might continue to position us in our modern context.

Christ's Political Achievement and Christ-Followers' Primary Allegiance

John spoke of Jesus in overtly political terms from the outset, naming Jesus "the ruler of the kings of the earth" who made John, John's readers, and the worldwide company of Christ-followers "a kingdom, priests to his God and Father, to whom be the glory and the power into the ages of ages" (Rev. 1:5–6 AT). From these opening announcements to the book's close, John calls Christ-followers "to alternative allegiance and alternative identity."[4] Those gathered in Ephesus or Smyrna or Pergamum might have been uncomfortable to hear such claims being spoken aloud, even in a private house, since the vast majority of their neighbors would have identified the emperor Domitian as the one who holds such dominion and would have acknowledged Rome's empire to extend over "every tribe and people and language and nation" (13:7).[5] But here, "honor and power" are ascribed to Jesus "into the ages of ages" (1:6 AT). Domitian is answerable to Jesus; Jesus's kingdom will outlast Rome's.

All who have been gathered under the lordship of Jesus now constitute an alternative "kingdom," one that stands alongside and will supersede the

4. Kraybill, *Apocalypse*, 21.

5. This is assuming the book was written at some point in Domitian's reign (81–96 CE). On the date of Revelation, see David A. deSilva, *Seeing Things John's Way: The Rhetoric of Revelation* (Westminster John Knox, 2009), 34–37, and *Discovering Revelation: Content, Interpretation, Reception* (Eerdmans, 2019), 35–39. The dynamics would not have been significantly different, however, if one were to opt for the principal alternative date of 69–70 CE.

"kingdom of the world" (11:15). While John, alongside other early Christian voices, affirms that Jesus "loves us and freed us from our sins" (Rev. 1:5 NRSV), the accent of Jesus's redemptive work falls on the establishment of this alternative kingdom and the "ransoming" of people from every demographic for this alternative kingdom (5:9–10). We see this group—those who would constitute the citizenry of the new Jerusalem, whose names are registered in the Lamb's scroll of life—again in 7:9–10:

> There was a great multitude that no one could count, from every nation, from all tribes and peoples and languages, standing before the throne and before the Lamb, robed in white, with palm branches in their hands. They cried out in a loud voice, saying, "Salvation belongs to our God who is seated on the throne and to the Lamb!"

As Nelson Kraybill rightly concludes, for John, "the *global* church, encompassing all who truly know and follow Jesus, is the Christian's most important place of belonging."[6]

In John's context, this awareness of the Christian movement as something that embraced people from many nations and languages was likely intended to encourage the small communities of Christ-followers in any given city that they were part of something much larger, a worldwide movement. They were not nearly the deviant and powerless minority that their neighbors would have had them believe. They were part of a political entity that would grow beyond the capacity of people to count, that would unite a greater variety of people across the ages than any empire had been able to unite by the usual means of conquest, coercion, and seduction.

John shared Daniel's conviction that every empire that arises will also fall and that the kingdom of God would supplant every nation-state (see Dan. 2:21, 36–45; 7:15–27). This is the essential plot of Revelation, the story of how "the kingdom of the world" becomes "the kingdom of our Lord and of his Messiah, and he will reign forever and ever!" (Rev. 11:15). The preservation of any particular empire is not the Christ-follower's highest priority. Living for the kingdom of God, and living as its loyal citizens, *is*. Indeed, to pray "may your kingdom come" (Matt. 6:10) is to declare a fundamental detachment from one's nation since one is praying for its displacement!

6. Kraybill, *Apocalypse*, 176 (emphasis original).

John would counsel, at the very least, keeping a certain mental and emotional distance from any state. American readers, for example, are reminded that their hope is not ultimately in America. For all America's strengths and potential, it is still another empire that will fall. If we identify America with our hope, we deny the hope that John, in concert with all the Scriptures that look forward to the kingdom of God, sets before us. We need, rather, "a hope which confronts the fallenness of the American principality; a hope . . . emancipated from moral naivete about any supposed unique destiny for the nation; a hope freed from vainglorious delusions that America is a holy nation."[7] The eventual decline and fall of America, moreover, is no setback to God's bringing about the consummation of the kingdom.

At the same time, John reminds us that our highest allegiance in the present is to the multinational, multilingual, multicultural body of people that Jesus has ransomed to constitute a kingdom for God (Rev. 5:9–10; 7:9–10), for these are the people who will be our fellow citizens "into the ages of ages." Embracing this conviction might move us to shift our interests and priorities away from those of the political party with which we identify toward the interests of our fellow-citizens of God's kingdom, whatever the political entity is in which they reside or which country they hail from. The first question I ask about a person might shift, for example, from "Is he or she in 'my' country legally?" to "Is he or she a fellow citizen of the kingdom of God, to which—and to whose citizens—we both owe our primary allegiance and who, therefore, has a claim on my care?" Such a shift is also a witness to the coming kingdom of God and to the Lamb's redeeming work throughout the world.

The manner in which John draws attention to the kingdom of God also calls us to examine the lines that partisan politics draw between and around certain people groups over against the lines that the population-ransoming work of Christ both draws and erases. This includes calling into question the tendency for political "tribalism," which leads many Christians to consider themselves more closely attached to and allied with the people of their political party than to other Christians whose consciences have led them to align with an opposing political party. John might have us instead keep in view that day when people ransomed from all manner of political parties will stand together in the one, unified kingdom of God—long after every nation that hosted those political parties has been buried in the sands of time—and

7. Stringfellow, *Ethic*, 155.

to approach the short-lived politics of the present from that standpoint, not least for the sake of the witness it would bear.

Recentering Christ-Followers on the Throne of God and of the Lamb

Even though John's pressing concern is to help his congregations see beyond the propaganda of empire and understand the implications of joining in the adulation of the emperor and the economy of Rome (Rev. 12:1–14:13; 17:1–19:10), his visions did not begin there—and this, as we saw, is highly significant. Whatever its power, wealth, and reach, Rome is not the center of the cosmos. God's throne—the throne that God now shares with God's Anointed One, Jesus—*is*. John would have his audiences take their bearing from *this* center, to see the powers of the moment from *this* vantage point (4:1–5:14). The reminder of God's place in the cosmos immediately relativizes all temporal powers and authorities.

Moreover, God is "the Almighty," the *Pantokratōr*. John introduced God as such at the outset of his work (1:8) and keeps this term prominently before his audiences throughout (4:8; 11:15; 15:3; 16:7; 19:6, 15; 21:22). While *Pantokratōr* is a frequent epithet of God in the Greek translation of the Jewish Scriptures (whether as a rendering of *S^{e}baoth* or *Shaddai*), the Christ-followers in Roman Asia could not help but hear a contrast with the *autokratōr*, the reigning Caesar, consistently named as such in inscriptions throughout their cities, whose stature is significantly diminished in the comparison. As Revelation's visions unfold, John underscores the smallness of all political and other authorities—"the kings of the earth, the potentates, the generals, the rich, the mighty" (Rev. 6:15 AT)—when set in comparison to God and God's Anointed. In the face of God and the Lamb coming in judgment, to satisfy their "wrath" in the face of the cumulative injustice perpetrated on their earth against their own creatures *by* their own creatures, these seemingly powerful political, military, and economic figures cry out to the hills and rocks in their abject terror and powerlessness to cover them and hide them (6:12–17). Whatever military power is enjoyed by nations that pride themselves on such strength, John shows his audiences that the power and the forces at God's disposal are exponentially greater and more fearsome (8:6–9:19).[8]

8. On Revelation and the dangers of militarism, see Greg Carey, *Rereading Revelation: Theology, Ethics, and Resistance* (Eerdmans, 2025), 153.

John might challenge Christians in America, for example, to remember that, while the American political scene is important, it does not enjoy ultimacy. The obsessive concerns and relentless agendas of one or the other major political parties are not the starting point for Christian engagement—though far too many Christians expressing themselves (and thus, "witnessing") on social media seem to model otherwise. Our fixed starting point is the throne of God and of God's Anointed, and the amplitude of the "babel" around us requires that we engage in continuous recalibration of our minds and intentions around the *proper* center. John would have us maintain the mental and emotional distance we need so as to remain centered on God, the Lamb, and *their* global agendas. He would have us approach our engagement in the "local" politics of the American scene from a firm grounding in *that* location. To the extent that we do so, and speak and act accordingly, we bear witness to the *Pantokratōr* to whom all owe their primary allegiance. To the extent that we allow ourselves to take our fundamental bearings from one or another political tribe, we have been drawn into one twenty-first-century equivalent of idolatry, giving primacy to circles and programs that are, at best, secondary.

The second scene at this cosmic center draws attention to a scroll in the right hand of God—a scroll that we learn is associated with the manifestation of God's judgments upon God's rebellious creation and the hastening of the transfer of the kingdom of this world to the kingdom of God—and raises the question, "Who is worthy to open the scroll and break its seals?" (5:2). After a dramatic silence, it is Jesus who is acclaimed to have "conquered, so that he can open the scroll and its seven seals" (5:5). Jesus's means of "conquering," of course, involved his giving over of his own life as a ransom (5:9–10). This is the pattern for "conquering" that John continues to hold up throughout Revelation. Holy ones participate in the defeat of Satan "because of the blood of the Lamb and the word of their testimony, and they loved not their lives even unto death" (12:11 AT). Those who stand before God and sing "the song of Moses . . . and the song of the Lamb" have conquered by their consistent resistance to the pressure to worship the beast and to receive the mark of allegiance to the beast (15:2–3). In John's vision, such consistent resistance would have also required preferring faithfulness to God and the Lamb to the preservation of their own lives (Rev. 12:11).

The Lamb's way of conquest, pursued by those who "follow the Lamb wherever he goes" (14:4), is the way of faithfulness in witness and in deed, in stark contrast to the beast's manner of conquering. When we finally encounter the Roman heads of state in Revelation 13, we find them exercising rule through military strength ("Who is like the beast, and who is able to wage war against him?" 13:4 AT), boastful demagoguery ("speaking big and slanderous words," 13:5 AT), and silencing the opposition ("it was granted to him to wage war against the holy ones and to conquer them," 13:7 AT).

In the vastly changed circumstances of the twentieth- and twenty-first-century American representative democracy, in which vocal Christians have penetrated the highest levels of government and occupy influential lobbies, John's vision of the means by which the Lamb has "conquered" and demonstrated his "worthiness"—and the contrast of this with the means employed by the beast and his allies—raises poignant questions. Christians in America have been increasingly attracted to using the coercive power of the state to implement some of their goals for changing the direction of American society—and they have claimed that they are, in fact, making headway for *God* by doing so. "Dominion theology" asserts that Christians are called to infiltrate society's multiple networks of power to use their control of those structures to advance a "Christian" agenda for the transformation of society. Whatever case is to be made for such approaches, John does not seem to lend it support. Is it because he could not envision the time when it would be possible? It is impossible to say. The testimony he has left, however, only commends following Jesus's example rather than relying on the coercive power of the state. In this, he would seem to be supported by a broader consensus among New Testament writers. As N. T. Wright and Michael Bird suggest,

> A good deal of the New Testament, following directly from the teaching and example of Jesus himself, is about the radical redefinition of power: power in weakness, power through humble service, power and indeed victory through self-sacrifice.[9]

How Christians promote their goals for human society is part of Christian witness, and John, at least, seems to suggest that those means should also bear witness to the character of Jesus and *his* manner of "conquering." Imitating the means employed by worldly powers, which all too often involves "pandering to political leaders so that they might let us share their podium,"[10] carries with it the threat (or perhaps the promise!) of finding ourselves entirely comfortable in Babylon's bed.

9. N. T. Wright and Michael Bird, *Jesus and the Powers* (Zondervan, 2024), 72.
10. Wright and Bird, *Jesus and the Powers*, 101.

Challenging the Use of Religion as Political Propaganda

We have closely studied Revelation as John's answer to Roman imperial ideology—what we might call the political propaganda of the first century—based on his convictions about God's character and rule and about the failure of Roman imperial rule to align with God's character and rule. The "gospel of Augustus and Roman rule" provided the all-important ideological legitimation of Roman rule, presenting it as an expression of the benevolent provision of the gods for the peaceful and prosperous ordering of human life, world without end, amen. To the extent that the population of the provinces embraced this mythology, those who were dominated would consent to continue to *be* dominated. It was therefore important for John to break any lingering spell—the "sorcery"—that this ubiquitous propaganda cast over Christ-followers and to do so in such a way that enabled steadfast resistance to what would prove, for several centuries at least, an undefeatable enemy of the Christian church and, thus, of the "kingdom of our Lord and of his Messiah" (Rev. 11:15).

Once again it is important to take stock of the distance at which any modern nation stands from the target of John's exposé. Christians in nations like North Korea face uncannily similar dynamics and endure coercive measures as severe as anything John foresaw. The situation in the United States is vastly different, of course, made even more complex by the once-popular ideology of being a distinctively "Christian nation"—an ideology that has been making a comeback in some circles of power and their supporters. Christ-followers enjoy the freedom (the political, economic, and social right) to live lives that reflect and bear witness to Christ's lordship. A major challenge in the present political climate, however, is to do so while maintaining critical distance from those very structures that we think we can manipulate to Christ's advantage, lest we find ourselves in bed once again with the domination systems of the world, their contaminating ideology, and their idolatrous claims on our allegiance. Howard-Brook and Gwyther perceptively remark that, in the First World context, "seduction, rather than the fear of persecution," presents the greater danger to Christ-followers.[11]

Many Christians in America have made common cause with a particular brand of Republicanism because they regard this as a means by which to channel the power of the state to enact what they perceive to be

11. Howard-Brook and Gwyther, *Unveiling Empire*, xxii–xxiii.

a "Christian" agenda for American society. Scenes of prominent Christian pastor-celebrities gathered around Donald Trump in the Oval Office, laying their hands on him in prayer; of Trump holding up a Bible in front of a church; of AI-engineered portraits of Jesus standing behind Trump on his knees, hands on Trump's shoulders, as if to steel him for the work ahead—these all function to give a political leader religious legitimacy as a divinely summoned political candidate and president using the language, practices, and images of Christianity.[12] John wrote in a context in which provincial elites led their neighbors to regard the Roman state and its rulers as divine. In our context, political-religious elites have led vast numbers of their political party to declare a political figure and his movement to be *instruments* of the divine. It is a strikingly similar dynamic, merely tailored to Christian monotheism. Either way, religion is being used to invest a political figure with divine support and purpose.

John's reaction to the use of religious language and forms to legitimate Roman power should give Christ-followers pause. John would caution Christians against the dangers of lending religious legitimation to political parties, personalities, and agendas without maintaining the distance that allows for both affirmation *and* critique, that continues to remind politicians of their accountability to God and God's vision for the holy and just use of power, both in terms of the means and the ends. Revelation also problematizes the absolute loyalty that some members of particular political parties, including many who identify themselves as Christians, demand and appear to enforce against any who voice criticism of the party's agenda and means to attain its goals. This is, rather, the loyalty that *all* Christians owe only to one regime—the kingdom of God and his Anointed, which will one day *supplant* the American state and any of its successors in the ongoing flow of history.

A significant number of Christians—and this appears to be more often the case for Christians who align with the political right—seem unaware of the danger, not to mention the irony, of turning "the kingdom of our Lord and of his Messiah" into a prop for the agenda of one political party in "the kingdom of the world," as if the latter had the real priority. Much of what the imperial cult accomplished in John's context is achieved in some American

12. This is not to be taken as a criticism of those who voted for Donald Trump per se. My concern here is with those who did so while failing to maintain the kind of critical distance that, I believe, John would have *all* Christ-followers preserve in regard to any and all political figures, as well as failing to maintain charity and respect toward their fellow Christ-followers and co-citizens for eternity whose consciences led them in other directions.

contexts using the language and trappings of Christian faith—lending religious legitimation to a political party and identifying support for that party's agenda with piety itself as if there were only one "Christian" choice at the polls.[13] Politicians foster these dynamics. They promise to advance longstanding interests of particular Christian voters and, in return, they are hailed and promoted as God's instruments and granted religious "cover" for whatever other agenda items they advance. John might well describe this kind of political alliance as "fornication," with the temporal power employing "sorcery"—deceptive wiles—to dupe Christ-followers. He might well indict prominent Christian leaders for playing the harlot, lending religious legitimation to the political agenda of political figures to enjoy the benefits of political patronage in return.

John would call Christ-followers to be careful about using the faith, which declares the lordship of Jesus and the impermanence of *all* temporal states, to deposit "religious capital into the coffers of political leaders."[14] At those specific points at which a party's agenda aligns with the righteous vision of God, Christians can affirm it. The fact, however, that so many American Christians can identify elements in the agendas of both major political parties that so align—and so many elements in the opposing party, at least, that fail so to align—should motivate all believers to embrace the critical distance from both parties that Revelation encouraged in regard to the only political force in his own setting. Regrettably, it has instead caused Christians to condemn their brothers and sisters whose consciences lead them to align with the opposing party.[15] Recovering the skill of *listening* to a broader swath of those people who will be fellow citizens with us forever in the kingdom of God could lead Christians in either camp to be more discerning about the underside of the party with which they have aligned—and to use their voices prophetically to call their own parties into closer alignment with the righteousness of God. John would have Christians obey the summons to serve as the conscience of the state (and of any particular party) rather than as cheerleaders.

Greg Carey has called attention to and questioned the appropriateness of John's use of the technique of "debasing" his opponents in Revelation,

13. Wright and Bird (*Jesus and the Powers*, 75) rightly affirm that "the Church does not exist to provide religious sponsorship to anyone's programmes."

14. Wright and Bird, *Jesus and the Powers*, 101.

15. Greg Carey (*Rereading Revelation*, 125) rightly affirms: "Faithfulness to Jesus ought not to be aligned with a partisan political agenda."

focusing particularly on John's treatment of the rival prophet whom he labels "Jezebel."[16] While I personally believe that Jezebel's teaching was genuinely harmful to Christian witness and posed a grave danger to her followers' spiritual well-being and Christian witness, the implications of Carey's critique for Christians in twenty-first-century America are important. Many believers have too quickly imitated John's tactics of debasing and demonizing the "other," generally in the interest merely of promoting or defending a political party's agenda. This serves the political beasts' purposes well, but it bears witness to the world that our allegiance to our party is more important than showing reverence for the Lord of the everlasting kingdom who commanded his citizens to love their neighbors as themselves, to love their enemies (which fellow Christians of any party, in any case, are *not*), and to avoid debasing speech as assiduously as avoiding murder (Matt. 5:21–22, 43–45; 22:37–40). Again, we would do better to listen to and be respectful of Christians not aligned with our own political outlook so as to preserve our own critical distance from the party seeking our complete and unquestioning allegiance and thus to preserve the possibility of serving as the conscience for that party.

The "Alternative Politics" of the Christian *Ekklēsiai*

John considered the Christian assemblies (*ekklēsiai*, Rev. 1:4) collectively to constitute the beginnings, at least, of "a kingdom" for the "God and Father" of Jesus Christ (1:6; see also 5:10). The early Christian leaders' decision to refer to gatherings of Christ-followers as *ekklēsiai* (rather than using terms already in widespread use among Jewish groups for such gatherings) aligns with John's explicitly political claim concerning their collective identity. "The Greek *ekklēsia* was an assembly, a coming together of people for political purposes. So, too, the Christian *ekklēsia* was expected to be the foundation for community life based on the principles expressed in the New Jerusalem vision"—and, one might add, the principles expressed throughout the instructions of Jesus and his envoys found in the New Testament.[17] These citizen assemblies of the "colonies" of the kingdom of God were small and relatively powerless throughout the first century, but they were nevertheless able to create networks of mutual aid and encouragement, as well as to support

16. Carey, *Rereading Revelation*, 23, 32.
17. Howard-Brook and Gwyther, *Unveiling Empire*, 192–93.

travel, communication, and even cooperation between colonies. There was a fledgling "politics" taking shape, and this internal politics, this *alternative* politics, also became a source of witness to the citizens of the Roman Empire.

John implicitly encouraged the assemblies of God's colonies in the seven cities of Roman Asia to invest themselves in doing what is righteous and just in God's sight. These righteous deeds would be the manner in which the bride, the new Jerusalem, prepared herself for the eschatological wedding to the Lamb. The "righteous deeds of the saints" constituted "the fine linen, bright and pure," with which the bride would adorn herself at her climactic manifestation at the end of history (Rev. 19:6–8). These same deeds would "follow" those who die in the Lord (14:13), existing forever in the adornment of the Christ-followers' forever home.

As the church's size and strength increased, so did the visibility of their collective mobilization to do what was righteous, good, and loving in the sight of their eternal ruler. The early Christians deplored the common practice of exposing unwanted infants, whose fate might be to be taken to be raised as slaves, to become prey for animals, or simply to die of exposure. They did not petition the imperial government to institute a change in the laws. Rather, they made it their collective practice to search out the places known as sites for such exposure and to adopt and raise the children they found (or else at least to tend them and give them an honorable burial if they were too far gone).[18] During a plague that struck Carthage in the mid-third century, Christians did not lobby the imperial government to retool the health-care system. Led by their bishop, Cyprian, they did the unthinkable and cared for the victims of the plague themselves, taking the sick into their own homes at tremendous risk to their own health. By the end of the third century, Christians had a reputation for the love that they cherished *and acted upon* in regard to one another and in regard to the vulnerable around them (see Tertullian, *Apology* 39). As Howard-Brook and Gwyther observe, "The communal context [of the *ekklesia*] created the possibility for an alternative reality."[19]

The church was not and *is* not limited in regard to its impact to what it can achieve by political means or through political involvement. In our changed situation, in which Christians account for 25 percent of the global population and, in the West at least, have great freedom and *significant* resources, Christians do not *have* to be absorbed with the political scene

18. Referred to in Wright and Bird, *Jesus and the Powers*, 65.
19. Howard-Brook and Gwyther, *Unveiling Empire*, 194.

and its polarizing clamor in order to do the work God has laid upon us and thereby have a profound impact on the lives of millions. The church, particularly if it is willing to work as a network of colonies of a single kingdom of God, can accomplish a great deal without any help from political authorities. This is not to be "apolitical," but to be "otherly political," to engage in our own constructive "politics" on behalf of the world and in service to God's agenda for human beings. This is not "building" the new Jerusalem. That falls under God's purview. But it is a powerful means of witnessing to the life of the kingdom to which we profess allegiance and in line with whose laws we are called to live now as we follow the instructions of Jesus and his ambassadors, the apostles. It is a means by which to anticipate the life of the kingdom of God and incarnate it in the present, however partially and temporarily. In so doing, we contribute to spinning the "fine linen" in which the bride will ultimately be arrayed.

We have need of visionary inspiration to imagine alternatives to the well-worn ruts of the society in which we live and that taught us to imagine only the possibilities that it allows—including the notion that any real social change has to happen by means of the powers and channels of the state. This is admittedly an area in which John offers less help, perhaps because John did not have the benefit of looking out over a world in which a full 25 percent of the population claims allegiance to Christ. As colonies of God's kingdom that now enjoy a considerable population with considerable wealth (and that are part of a *global* network of such colonies that makes a mockery of the power of national borders to constrain Christian interest and involvement), of what "righteous deeds" are we truly capable? What infrastructures could we create, quite apart from goading our governments, to address the pressing human needs that we identify?

Revelation defines the task of churches in the United States to be to recover their identity *not* as gatherings of American Christianity but as colonies of the kingdom of God, the vanguard not of a return to a "Christian America" but the vanguard of the Christ whose "kingdom does not belong to this world" (John 18:36) but that, we fervently pray, will one day supplant *all* the kingdoms of this world, including the nation we call "America."

The Larger Call to "Witness" in Revelation

John's primary summons to his congregations was to maintain a clear and uncompromised witness, in both word and practice, to the sovereign rule of the one and only God; to the redemptive, kingdom-creating acts of Jesus Messiah; and to the allegiance and obedience that are due God as Creator and to God's Anointed as redeemer and chosen co-regent.[20] This witness required maintaining a critical distance from the propaganda that legitimated and the practices that expressed partnership with any and every power and practice that was not aligned with the righteous decrees of God and God's Anointed. Throughout Revelation, John particularly arouses emulation of, or association with, those who bear witness, whether Jesus (1:5; 2:14), John himself (1:2, 9), Antipas (2:13), the two witnesses (11:3–13), or those who maintained the "witness of Jesus" (12:17; see also 12:11 CEB).[21] Witness (and God's vindication of the faithful witnesses who testify to God and what is due God to the point of their deaths) emerges as the only efficacious path to provoking recognition of God among the inhabitants of the earth. God's visitations of judgment do not bring about repentance and recognition of God (9:20–21)—indeed, they even provoke the opposite (16:9, 11, 21). It is only God's witnesses and God's follow-up actions in the wake of witness that move "the inhabitants of the earth" to revere God and give him honor (11:13).

Revelation summons us to consider what is the "witness" that we must bear in our contemporary setting. The typical answer would be that Christians in any setting ought to be prepared to "share the gospel." This is a fine response *if* we are prepared to understand "the gospel" as John would understand it. The gospel, for him, includes a call to allegiance to the one who is "ruler of the kings of the earth" (Rev. 1:5) and to obey the commandments of God, the one whose enthronement is forever, above those of any political entity. We bear this witness when we set loyalty to Christ and to the global citizenship of Christ's kingdom as our first priority and give voice to this priority when considering issues of immigration, foreign aid, and persecuted populations requiring intervention. We bear this witness when we maintain our solidarity with Christians of any and all political parties rather than allow party lines to introduce enmity into the body of Christ.

John himself modeled witnessing also to the distance between the political, economic, policing, and ideological practices he observed in Roman Asia (and empire wide) and the values and practices promoted in the scriptures. He did this, in all likelihood, not with the hope that Roman officials or merchants or demagogues would change their practices but rather with the

20. See Brian K. Blount, *Witness*, 38, 46–47; *Revelation: A Commentary* (Westminster John Knox, 2009), 118; deSilva, *Seeing Things*, 69–72, 331.

21. See further, deSilva, *Seeing Things*, 222–27.

hope of alerting Christ-followers to disengage from all practices the one God would consider unjust—and would judge (see Rev. 18:4). We, too, are to bear witness to God's righteousness and to the unrighteousness of policies and practices that violate human dignity, that replicate the economic exploitation practiced by the empires condemned in our Scriptures, that protect the privilege of the few at the expense of the needs of the many. And just as the prophets of old reserved their fiercest critiques for their own people, calling them to repentance and to a fresh alignment with God's vision for human community, so we are called to do the same within our own political "tribes."

Most of all, we are called, as citizens of a kingdom yet to break fully into the history of this world, to live together in constructive ways that bear witness to that kingdom's ruler and that kingdom's laws and values—and, by doing so, make the desirability of belonging to that kingdom apparent to those who have not embraced Christ or who have lost the hope that God has extended to the world in Christ. John's closing vision of the new Jerusalem presents human society organized with God—God's reign, God's light, God's justice—at the center of all things. John has never seen anything like this in life, not in Rome, not in Ephesus, not even in Jerusalem. New Jerusalem is not "brought about by famine and war and pestilence and natural disaster."[22] It is prepared as the people of God engage the acts of justice and righteousness that spin the fine linen in which the bride is robed. It is built on the foundations of the apostles (Rev. 21:14), not on the foundations of violence or greed, but on the gospel of the truth of God. The new city exists to bring peace and healing to the nations (22:2), rather than to establish "peace" by controlling, dominating, and subduing. The city faces no threat (the gates are never shut, 21:25). Military conquest, international strife, struggles for maintaining a balance of power are all done away with in this vision. Resources are expended no longer in futile wars and power struggles but rather for the well-being of all.

In the end, only God and God's Anointed can usher in the consummate reign of God. All we can do is witness to that reign by speaking and living together in ways aligned now with God's reign. New Jerusalem is a costly alternative. One cannot profit from Babylon's partnership, violence, and falsehoods and still expect a welcome in the new Jerusalem (21:8, 27). We cannot legitimate, either by our participation or by our silence, our society's

22. Against the claim made by Tina Pippin, *Death and Desire: The Rhetoric of Gender in the Apocalypse of John* (Westminster John Knox, 1992), 102–3.

failure to enact God's righteousness, however it manifests itself. John urges disciples to learn how to live as aliens in a land that is not our own, looking away to our native land, the city that none of us has yet seen but that is the consummation of the great story of God.

> *Now, in the meanwhile, with hearts raised on high,*
> *We for that country must yearn and must sigh;*
> *Seeking Jerusalem, dear native land,*
> *Through our long exile on Babylon's strand.*[23]

Even so, come, Lord Jesus.

23. This is a verse from the twelfth-century hymn "O quanta qualia sunt illa Sabbata," written by Peter Abelard, as translated from Latin into English by John M. Neale, *The Hymnal Noted* (London, 1854).

For Further Reading

Blount, Brian K. *Revelation: A Commentary*. Westminster John Knox, 2009. A very readable yet richly detailed commentary, appropriate for pastors (all the more as the author is an accomplished preacher).

Boxhall, Ian. *The Revelation of Saint John*. Hendrickson, 2006. Another readable commentary well within the grasp of pastors and motivated laity, particularly rich in laying out correspondences with ancient literature.

Carey, Greg. *Rereading Revelation: Theology, Ethics, and Resistance*. Eerdmans, 2025. A thoughtful and sensitive introduction to the message of Revelation, the ethical issues raised by the text (and in the interpretation of the text), and the challenge of Revelation in a contemporary Western context.

Carey, Greg. *Ultimate Things: An Introduction to Jewish and Christian Apocalyptic Literature*. Chalice, 2005. A fine introduction to the apocalyptic genre and mindset, and to the larger body of literature that constitutes this genre.

deSilva, David A. *Archaeology and the Book of Revelation: A Visual Guide*. Baker Academic, 2026. A guide to the archaeological and other material remains that illuminate the late first-century lived environment of the seven cities whose Christian residents were addressed by John, along with Patmos and Rome, enhanced by almost 250 full-color photographs. The whole is attentive to how immersion in these environments illumines reading Revelation alongside its original audiences.

deSilva, David A. *Discovering Revelation: Content, Interpretation, Reception*. Eerdmans, 2019. An introduction to the message and interpretation of the whole text of Revelation with special emphasis on how the book has been interpreted at different moments in the history of the church.

deSilva, David A. *A Week in the Life of Ephesus*. IVP Academic, 2020. A historical novel set late in 89 CE providing an imaginative context for hearing Revelation's message and challenge in the city of Ephesus, punctuated by nonfiction sidebars introducing facets of the culture and environment.

Duvall, J. Scott. *The Heart of Revelation: Understanding the 10 Essential Themes of the Bible's Final Book*. Baker Books, 2016. An accessible introduction to Revelation's contributions to reflection on major topics and themes of Scripture, including God, Jesus, worship, the people of God, mission, judgment, and perseverance.

Hemer, Colin J. *The Letters to the Seven Churches of Asia in Their Local Setting*. JSOT Press, 1986. A now-classic study of the historical settings of the seven churches and the potential impact of local knowledge on the interpretation of Revelation.

Howard-Brook, Wes, and Anthony Gwyther. *Unveiling Empire: Reading Revelation Then and Now*. Orbis, 1999. A reading of Revelation as a challenge to political and economic domination systems, ancient and modern.

Keener, Craig S. *Revelation*. New International Version Application Commentary. Zondervan, 2000. An accessible commentary by a leading evangelical scholar, particularly interested in bridging the horizons between John's setting and our own.

Koester, Craig R. *Revelation*. Yale University Press, 2014. A richly detailed and historically grounded commentary on Revelation, with particular attention to its history of interpretation. Given its density and detail, this is most appropriate for more advanced students of Revelation.

Koester, Craig R. *Revelation and the End of All Things*. Eerdmans, 2001. A fine discussion of the role of Revelation in Christian eschatology as well as a mini-commentary on Revelation itself, read from the perspective of the original audience.

Kraybill, J. Nelson. *Apocalypse and Allegiance: Worship, Politics, and Devotion in the Book of Revelation*. Brazos, 2010. An excellent introduction to the Roman imperial context of Revelation, particularly in its political and economic aspects, laced with challenging insights into Revelation's illumination of the modern context of America and faithful response therein.

Maier, Harry O. *Apocalypse Recalled: The Book of Revelation After Christendom*. Fortress, 2002. An insightful and also deeply personal reflection on Revelation's challenge to first-century Christians and, on this basis, its challenge to Christians in the twenty-first century. Another excellent example of how to bridge those horizons responsibly and perceptively.

McKnight, Scot, with Cody Matchett. *Revelation for the Rest of Us: A Prophetic Call to Follow Jesus as a Dissident Disciple*. Zondervan, 2023. A vibrantly written introduction to a historically grounded reading of Revelation that is equally interested in drawing out the book's implications for faithful witness and faithful living in the modern context.

Mounce, Robert H. *The Book of Revelation*. Revised edition. New International Commentary on the New Testament. Eerdmans, 1997. A solid commentary on Revelation for pastors and teachers.

Stewart, Alexander E., and Alan S. Bandy, eds. *The Apocalypse of John Among Its Critics: Questions & Controversies*. Lexham, 2023. A thoughtful collection of essays introducing a number of facets of Revelation that have provoked strong criticism among scholars and other readers (its violence, its presentation of women and of female figures, its presentation of Jews, its intolerance) and evaluating these criticisms in light of John's context and purposes.

White, C. Dale. *Making a Just Peace: Human Rights & Domination Systems*. Abingdon, 1998. An excellent primer on the ways in which systems take on an oppressive life of their own and enlist the unwitting support and acceptance of human participants.

Wilson, Mark W. *Revelation*. Zondervan Illustrated Bible Backgrounds Commentary. Zondervan, 2007. A judiciously illustrated introduction to the archaeological, geographical, and cultural world of Roman Asia Minor and reading Revelation in its historical context.

Witherington, Ben, III. *Revelation*. Cambridge University Press, 2003. An accessible commentary on reading Revelation in its historical context by a leading New Testament scholar deeply committed to the life of the church.

Index of Ancient Sources

Extrabiblical Literature

Color Gallery

FIGURE 2.4. The Acropolis of Pergamum. See page 16 for more information.

FIGURE 2.5. Friedrich Thiersch's 1882 reconstruction of the Acropolis of Pergamum. See page 17.

FIGURE 2.6. The site of the Altar of Zeus, overlooking Pergamum/Bergama. See page 17.

FIGURE 2.7. The monumental Altar of Zeus as reconstructed in the Pergamon Museum. See page 18.

FIGURE 2.10. Temple of Julius Caesar and Artemis, Ephesus. See page 20.

FIGURE 2.12. Remains of altar from the Temple of Domitian. See page 21.

FIGURE 3.13. The once grand staircase giving access to the sacred precinct of the Domitian temple. See page 43.

FIGURE 3.14. Remains of the colossal statue of Domitian (Titus?) from the Flavian temple in Ephesus. See page 43.

FIGURE 3.17. Temple of Trajan and Zeus, Pergamum. See page 46.

FIGURE 3.20. An inscription made by "the council and citizenry of the first and great metropolis of Asia and twice *neōkoros* city of the Ephesians." See page 47.

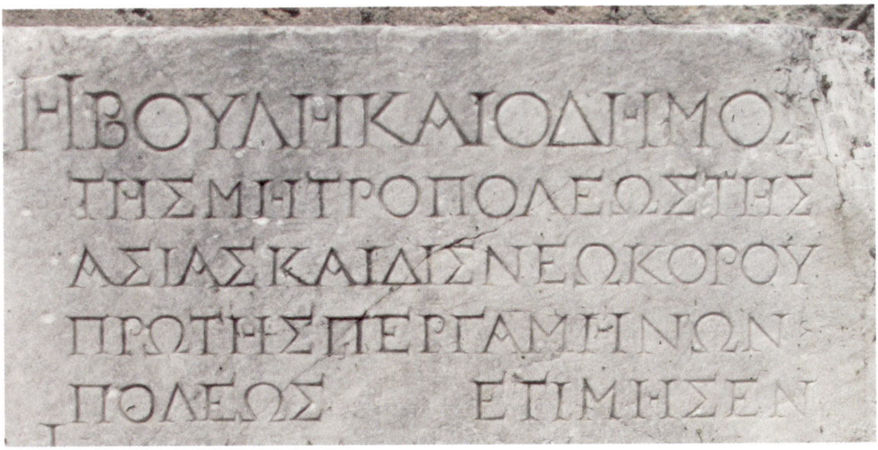

FIGURE 3.21. An inscription from the Asklepion outside of Pergamum. See page 47.

FIGURE 4.3. *The Whore of Babylon* (1809) by William Blake. See page 68.

FIGURE 3.23. Sesterce of Vespasian; reverse showing the goddess Roma seated and reclining on Rome's seven hills. See page 50.

FIGURE 6.1. Denarius ofTitus; reverse showing facade of the Temple of Jupiter on the Capitoline Hill. See page 101.

FIGURE 2.2. Silver cistophorus (tetradrachm) ofClaudius; reverse showing the cult statue of Diana (Artemis). See page 15.

FIGURE 4.2. A statue of Apollo from the Vatican Museums. See page 55.